Love and Trauma

A MEMOIR OF A SMALL GIRL WHO GREW UP

Mila Sharma

Copyright © 2022 Mila Sharma

All right reserved. No part of this book may be reproduced, distributed, or transmitted in any form by any means without the permission of the publisher, except by a reviewer, who may quote brief passages in a review.

This book is a memoir and reflects the author's present recollections of experiences over time. Some names have been changed, events have been compressed, and dialogue has been added.

The resources in this book are provided for informational purposes only and should not be used to replace medical advice. The intent is to provide general information to help the reader gain spiritual awareness. You may use any of this information in this book for yourself, the author and the publisher cannot be held responsible for the use of the information provided in this book.

Front cover photo provided by Pixabay©
Edited by Mila R. Sharma

1st Edition

ISBN 978-1-7780948-2-8 (Hardcover)

ISBN 978-1-7780948-3-5 (Paperback)

ISBN 978-1-7780948-1-1 (ebook)

Libraries and Archives Canada Cataloguing in Publication

1. Inspiration & Personal Growth 2. Abuse/Child Abuse 3. Personal Memoir 4. Angels & Spirit Guides l. Sharma, Mila 1987-

Some will not like me for this.

Others will not know how to react.

The rest will embrace me for my courage.

Dedicated to all the Baby Mila's of the world. Know that it gets better. Trust yourself and surrender all that you cannot control to the universe. Above all, never stop loving yourself!

"There are no accidents. And if there are, it is up to us to look at them as something else. And that bravery is what creates flowers."

— Prince Rogers Nelson

Contents

Introduction	1
1. Between 2 Homes	3
2. Traumas and Wishes	7
3. Trauma is a vicious cycle	9
4. You are not the only one	13
5. My first experience	17
6. When life became shit	21
7. The start of the abuse	23
8. It is not your fault	29
9. L.O.V.E.	33
10. Who am I?	39
11. Anger (Part 1)	45
12. Forgiveness	53
13. Consequences	59
14. Truth	65

15.	Reflections	73
16.	Burden	79
17.	Therapies	83
18.	Sabotage	89
19.	Working with Baby Mila	93
20.	Courage	97
21.	Letting go	99
22.	My fear of men	103
23.	Strong female influences	107
24.	Putting in the work	113
25.	My soulmate	119
26.	My dreams	125
27.	Find what makes you happy	131
28.	How I met my Spirit Guides	135
29.	Surrender	139
30.	The Moon	141
31.	Anger (Part 2)	145
32.	My intention and hope	149
33.	My sincere gratitude	151
Epilogue		157
Acknowledgments		161

Introduction

As I write these words on paper, I can already feel tears forming in my eyes. It is getting tough to swallow because a ball of fear is stuck in the pit of my throat. I am afraid to open up. Afraid to speak my truth. Afraid to talk about what really happened.

This book discusses the traumas that I have faced and experienced. Traumas that no one human being should ever have to experience, but it happens. No longer should we be afraid to speak up and say that this feels wrong. It is wrong. You are wrong. Abuse is wrong.

It took me over thirty years to even acknowledge what happened to me. For years, I drowned my sorrows in a bottle just to swallow the guilt and hide my shame. Always smiling and sharing what light I had with the world. No one would ever suspect that I was once a victim but spoiler alert—I survived. I made it through. I did that.

Now that small light that I used to share with the world has now illuminated my inner mind and body. I am no longer a victim. I am a SURVIVOR. I am LOVE and LIGHT.

This book is dedicated to anyone who has been made to feel small like they were not good enough and would never amount to anything. It is also dedicated to those who have suffered from any abuse, whether it be sexual, physical, emotional, or mental. It is for anyone still looking for absolution. It is possible and I am here to help.

This book was written based on my own experiences with trauma and what I learned during my healing processes. In no way does this reflect the end all be all on how to heal. You will learn what works for you through your own trial and error. We all have a journey and a conclusion. What will yours be?

Chapter One

Between 2 Homes

Growing up, I never knew where I belonged. At school, I could never figure out whether I was accepted by the geeks, the cool kids, or the in-betweeners. I guess I floated between the cliques, more of a loner than anything. Perhaps, I never quite knew where I belonged because I did not even know where I belonged in my own family.

I have both biological and guardian parents. I was born in Prince George, British Columbia—the greatest small town (at least to me!). A month later, I would move to Burnaby, in Metro Vancouver, with my biological parents. Only to find out my dad had lost his job (before I was born) and it was getting challenging to find someone to take care of me, my older brother, and my sister.

I should probably explain how my guardian parents were chosen. My biological dad's older brother married my biological mom's older sister. Conveniently, my biological parents met at their wedding, fell in love, and years later got married.

Throughout this book, I will be referring to my biological parents as my family and my guardian family as my Prince George family.

With the status of my dad being unemployed and unable to find work, my Prince George family had made a promise to my parents that if they ever needed any support, they would be there. My parents trying their hardest not to take them up on their offer had to make the difficult decision on whether or not they should send me to Prince George. In their minds, it would have been best to keep me.

However, given my parent's financial situation at the time, they thought it would be better to send their daughter to live with extended family rather than a random babysitter. So, the night before Christmas Eve, my parents decided to send me to Prince George until they were able to get back on their feet. My brother and sister remained in Burnaby as they were older and were able to walk and talk; whereas, myself being a newborn, I had no capacity for any of that.

On Christmas Eve, I was taken back to Prince George on a plane at ten months old with my dad's younger brother to live with my Prince George parents, along with their two daughters and son (my cousins), and my grandfather (dad's father). Little did I know that I would have the most wonderful childhood as well as experience some of the darkest traumas. But we will save that for later.

My parents were quite different than my Prince George family. My parents were struggling to survive. Trying to make sure that there was enough money for food, a house, and necessities but lacked the love and communication that I would find in Prince George with my other family.

I lived in Prince George for about nine years, with random periods when my parents would try to take me back to live with them in Burnaby and re-acquaint me with my brother and sister. It never worked.

I did not even know that my parents were my parents until I was two years old. We spent holidays and summers together as a joint family, but when I was finally forced to move to Burnaby at nine years old, that was the end of my happy times. Life got real and the physical and emotional abuse got even more real.

I no longer had my Prince George family to keep me safe or to sing me songs to sleep at night.

Now it was 'do what you are told and do not talk back'. Do not say 'NO' or you get smacked. My supports were gone. My brother and sister did not acknowledge or speak up for me. My brother who had been the primary victim of the physical and emotional abuse before I came to live there was now no longer the victim. I became the target for everyone. Had a tough day? Let us take it out on Mila. Stressed out? Let us take it out on Mila. Feeling bad about yourself? Let us take it out on Mila.

Trying to sneak phone calls to my Prince George family was difficult and often monitored. Letters were read or thrown out before they could be sent. Maybe because they were all about me wanting to move back and how I hated my new home. For years, I cried myself to sleep and would then get in trouble for crying. I was not supposed to be sad. My tears and emotions eventually dried up and I was no longer the free-spirited child that I was once destined to be.

Chapter Two

Traumas and Wishes

When you are a child, you never know why things are the way they are. As a child, we strive to be loved and taken care of. We want to laugh and have fun. We want to be free and enjoy the little things in life.

At the same time, we rush to grow up, not realizing that our rush to grow up would bring more responsibilities and harbour unseeded traumas that we maybe did not know existed. Only to realize that something might have happened to us when we get uneasy with a glance, a touch, a scent, a dream, or a memory that just pops out of no-where.

It might also just be that trauma that happened to us a long time ago that we never told anyone about. Well, it is coming back to us, but this time with pain, chronic injuries, inflammation, anxiety, depression, or macular holes in your eyes.

For years, I never dealt with my traumas—I never knew that I could. I was never taught that. I just thought that I had to be a good Indian girl and go through the motions of cleaning, cooking, and not talking back. Eventually, in my mind, I would be married at nineteen to my Prince Charming, and he would free me from my pain and misery. For years, I waited for Prince Charming to arrive, but he never came. I thought a few times I might have found him, but no—false alarm.

Do I still wait for my Prince Charming to show up on his white horse? Of course. But I have also realized that not only could I be my own Princess, but I could be my own Prince Charming that frees myself from the castle.

You cannot wait for someone to save you. Trauma will still follow you and turn your life upside down until you save and free yourself. Only then will your real king or queen show up for you.

Chapter Three

Trauma is a vicious cycle

They say that most forms of abuse stem from those who have gone through it before you and then those before them, and so on—many generations. It is almost like the gift that keeps on giving, even though it is far from any gift that anyone wants to receive.

The point is the person who is inappropriately touching you or hitting you may have been a victim of the abuse before. Everyone reacts and feels things differently. It is what they learned. They probably even made a vow, to themselves promising themselves that they will no longer be a victim. And if you think about it, they do just that. They stop being the victim as soon as they start being the perpetrator.

Now, they have control. They dictate the situation. There is no one to tell them otherwise. Worse, being a victim of the past means that they know just what you might say before you say it. So, they know just how to put you in place now as the abuser. Whatever they experienced in the past, is exactly what they are doing to you now—if not worse. All because they never chose to deal with their own traumas. Thus, continuing the generational chain of abuse.

Remember if it is happening to you then the chances of it having happened to them are likely. Of course, not all abusers have a history of being a victim. Some do it because they want that sense of power. Perhaps they are failing in other aspects of their life and want that control to survive. Even though they might know what they are doing is wrong, they continue to do it, so, why stop? The pleasure is too alluring. The power is too much of a thrill or adrenaline rush. A secret that only they and you know about.

So, who is going to tell on them? They hold all the cards. They make you believe that you cannot do better. Otherwise, if you leave, you will not be loved. You have no escape—they are your escape.

No longer will I be a victim. Instead, I am going to break and end the cycle. I am going to survive and heal. I am more than capable. I am strength. I am love and light.

Chapter Four

You are not the only one

Growing up, I always thought that I was the only one being abused. But now when I look back on it, the abuse happened to others as well.

My dad mentally and emotionally abused my mom by making her feel like she was not good enough or could never be enough. Nothing positive, just hurtful words. Probably, stemming from the loss of his mother at a young age, and being raised by a father who did not see him with the same level of worth as his other children. His lack of love eventually led him to use his power to compensate for what he lacked in his upbringing within his own family.

My dad hit my brother before I came into the picture. When it stopped for my brother, it started for me.

I always thought that my male cousin in Prince George was only sexually abusing me, but it turns out that he was doing the same to my brother as well. It is sad how when one abuse stops, another is experienced and gained.

I found out seven years ago that my brother had been sexually abused as a child when he finally came out about it. At the time, I did not know how to react. I sure as hell did not come out and say 'Yes, that happened to me too!' Instead, I stayed quiet. Even the email my brother sent to the family sharing his story of the sexual abuse that he endured, I never read. I did not want to relive what I had gone through. So, I again stayed quiet.

As we grew up, my brother became increasingly reactive, abusive, and a bully, likely because of the abuse he underwent. My brother and I have always had a rocky and limited relationship because of my connection with my Prince George family due to the sexual abuse committed by their son. However, at no point did my brother ever ask me if the sexual abuse happened to me too.

My brother is forever a victim, but I am proud of him for speaking his truth. I just wish that he was able to get the resolution he needed to overcome his trauma. As far as I know, he is still coping with his vices and has not started his healing journey. I hope that this book finds him well and gives him another outlook on life.

Looking back, I think that if I had spoken up about what I went through when my brother did, it would have taken away from him being center stage. Also, I might have gotten dragged down with him and my dad to cope how only they knew how: to drink. Ultimately, I was not ready to face that abuse. To me, I thought it was the lesser of the other abuses. Truthfully, this one did not leave me in tears, bruises, or goose eggs.

Chapter Five

My first experience

I was twenty-five years old. I met him in Las Vegas. He was there for a bachelor party which ironically happened to be his own.

Day one, we met at a nightclub.

Day two, we ended up running into each other at another nightclub in the centre of a crowded dance floor. The chemistry was undeniable and the feelings were mutual. I am a firm believer in destiny and fate, and to me, this seemed like fate. At the time, I was just embracing life, not thinking about my actions or the repercussions. But whatever it was, it felt good.

Day three, we collectively met as a group and went out. One thing led to another on the dance floor. At first, we were with our group and then we were in a different section, staring into each others' eyes and passionately kissing. It was the first time I had let myself truly live in the moment. The kiss led us down a dark hallway until it led us out of the club and onto the main strip. Still lost and mesmerized, we walked to his hotel room and that is when it happened.

At twenty-five years old, I was no longer a virgin. It was not like I wanted to have sex with him, but it got to the point where I felt like I was obligated to please the man, so to speak. The deed was done.

It was then that he decided to unleash all his feelings on how he felt about his own life and of me. To him, our meeting was far from coincidental but neither of us made a move to make a future plan.

At the time, I did not know what I was feeling other than comforted. Was this my true love? I let him spill his feelings and I just smiled. It was not until after the trip that those feelings got stuck in my head and I was lost.

Once again, I would go through another secret struggle. No one to tell my secret to without being judged for my actions of being with an 'almost' married man.

Did I regret it? That is a tough question because the period after this was difficult. Another person who ultimately rejected me. My truthful answer though is I did not.

Everything happens as it is supposed to. The Universe or Spirit places us into situations like this to learn something. It then becomes our choice to go through with it, and hopefully, learn from it. I learned to never fall for the bachelor at his own party, and that I was deserving and capable of finding true love.

Little did I know that true love would be an indicator of me loving myself. But first I needed to lose myself even more.

Chapter Six

When life became shit

There are many years in my life that I would say that my life was shit but I think these years top it.

I am a Registered Nurse by trade, and in 2015 I was working with a patient, trying to ambulate him from his bedside commode to his bed. He was legally blind, had one functional leg, and was 250+ pounds. He was angry with life and upset with the doctors. The transfer back to the bed did not go according to plan with my colleague. I injured my back, neck, and shoulders. I was out of nursing for seven months—only to go back to work and to get injured again, and out for another several months.

I have experienced physical pain since my early teenage years from dance. Sometimes the pain would randomly manifest itself in my ankles and hips. Apparently, once you have longstanding pain that becomes chronic, it takes much longer to heal new injuries than someone with no history of chronic pain. Needless to say, my pain is still here, and it manifested itself in other areas of my body—including my eyes.

The pain that should have healed did not. No matter how many massages I received, how much physiotherapy I underwent, or how many acupuncture appointments I went to. My pain remained.

It was not until 2018 that my mom suggested that I try Reiki, a traditional Japanese healing modality that allows energy to flow and promotes the clearing of any blocks that may be impeding the flow. My mom, being a victim of chronic pain and who was also moving towards her own enlightenment, pushed me towards more holistic medical approaches. So, on May 20th, 2018, I became a Level 1 Reiki Practitioner. I healed my plantar fasciitis and chronically sprained ankles.

But the pain elsewhere kept getting worse and I kept getting better at concealing it. Hardly anyone around me knew how much I was suffering. To them, I was the girl who always had her makeup done and a smile on her face. You would never know if she was coming or going. That was me—and then I had my breakdown.

Chapter Seven

The start of the abuse

From what I can remember about my own abuse, it started when I was two years old. I was molested by my older cousin (the son of my Prince George parents), who would have been eleven years old at the time. It started with kindness and love, all a secret and a game. I was sworn not to tell anyone, and for thirty-one years I stayed silent until I told my first boyfriend about it. Unable to go into details and still in shock about my brother. I had to tell someone, but hey, that is the first step, right? To speak about it.

The abuse happened when no one was around and with the door closed. No one in the family ever questioned anything. My male cousin was as nice as pie, never talked back, and was quiet, and sensitive. Even though what was happening to me was wrong, I never knew better. A small child's brain barely developed, and now was given the task to do adult things and play a secret game. What else could a child want?

By the age of three, I started developing hair under my armpits and on my genitals. I was taken to a multitude of doctors and not one suggested that the cause could be sexual abuse. Instead, the doctors gave me a diagnosis of having imbalanced hormones, where my body developed prematurely. I was living in a small town with a nice family—who would have suspected, otherwise?

Eventually, I went to the BC Children's Hospital in Metro Vancouver, for an endocrinologist appointment with my parents. The doctor did her assessment and said that the only way that this could have happened to me, to go through puberty this early *(and if it was not because of the imbalanced hormones)* was if there had been sexual contact with another individual. And that this sexual contact would have had to include genital to genital contact—and was likely done by a left-handed person. There are only two left-handed people in my family: my male cousin and me.

My parents did not think that sexual abuse could have been possible and assumed that the doctors knew best. Besides what would have prompted my parents to assume differently? They sent me (their daughter) to live with their trusted family

THE START OF THE ABUSE

(my dad's older brother and my mom's older sister) where you would never expect this type of abuse to be occurring. No one put two and two together. So again, I was sent back to Prince George to be abused under the radar by my male cousin.

I still remember that conversation with the doctor that I had as a child. What I cannot remember is if someone asked if anyone was touching me in areas that they should not have been. If she did, I likely would have said no. But how is a child supposed to feel comfortable enough to be open when their father and mother are both present in the room, and your underwear is off, and you have just been physically assessed by the doctor?

Not only was I being physically touched and forced to perform adult tasks by my male cousin, but I was constantly stuck going to doctors. Only to take my clothes off and have my private parts looked at. However, this time by a trained professional with their fingers and instruments. If one was not traumatizing enough on its own, then the other one raised the bar.

The abuse continued after my male cousin would get home from school or when I had to be put to bed (he would offer to do it). One time my female cousin, his sister, walked into the room, and I quickly jumped off the bed so that he could get himself back into his pants. Surprised that I was still awake. She did not question what was going on, no one did. I kept his secret.

Perhaps, subconsciously, I was trying to preserve our relationship and protect the image of myself, him, and my family. As far as I was concerned, at the time, no one needed to know.

Had my brother not come out about his own sexual abuse, I do not know if I would have told my boyfriend out of pure and utter shock. I guess when I would go visit our sister, my brother would visit our male cousin. I was the full-time victim, and my brother would be the vacation or part-time one.

It took me a long time to tell my sister what had happened to me. Part of me knew that if I did not tell her then she would not have been able to get over her own previous trauma with our mom's father. I wanted to tell her of my experience to help her get over her own sexual abuse that started from the age of eleven to fifteen years old.

Even though I told her about my situation, I never went into detail. To her, she thought it was a one-time thing. To me, the sexual abuse happened repeatedly, but I never wanted to make my problems seem worse than anyone else's. In the end, I wanted her to know that there would be light at the end of her struggle and that we would both get over this hurt and heal together.

H ealing is possible. It is the forgiveness and self-acceptance part that is hard.

Chapter Eight

It is not your fault

I never asked to be abused. Does anyone? But I was abused in more ways than one. Sometimes we grow up in families or situations as part of our karma or purpose. Somehow at the end of all this, it is our responsibility to figure out why we were put through this trauma, and what are the lessons we learned?

Trauma is a big word. It can mean many things. Some traumas can result from a fall or a spontaneous pneumothorax (collapsed lung). Others can be less obvious, like someone belittling you or telling you it is okay if you do this—it will make us both feel better. To overcome our trauma, it then becomes our job to try and dissect the trauma into tangible parts, so that we can accept what happened and heal, little by little.

Like I said before, for a time, I did not know we could heal from trauma. I thought we just had to silently swallow our shame and guilt and keep moving. At least that is what I learned and saw from my own parents.

No one in my family talked about any of this. And when I tried, I was shut down because we were not allowed to talk about the past. It made my dad feel like too much of a coward for physically and emotionally breaking down his own child, because of his insecurities and unhealed traumas. But when my brother came out about his sexual abuse, it was all we ever talked about.

Somewhere along the line, we need to realize that being abused is not our fault. Someone putting you in a situation where you could not use your voice—it is not your fault. Someone raising their hand to you—it is not your fault. You were just an innocent child that someone took advantage of, an easy target because not only are you smaller but you can easily be manipulated and silenced.

Most perpetrators probably do not even think about the long-term effects. That is if they even care to. But hey, look at them—they had upgraded from being a victim to being the one who victimizes others. They gained their power back, but not the way that they should have.

Chapter Nine
L.O.V.E.

Love. Love. Love.

What does love mean to me? Love should be warm, nice, supportive, present, beautiful, and kind. Love can also be patience or a lush caress until you are ready to move forward. My definition of love has been misconstrued from the beginning.

I suppose my upbringing with my Prince George family initiated my understanding of love. But somewhere down the road of their 'love' for me as a child and being loved in another way at two years old, became disjointed. It was confusing how experiencing something as bad as sexual abuse could also make me feel needed and cared for. At the time, I did not hate what I was made to do.

Looking back on it now, it makes me angry and enraged that I endured that for as long as I did.

But back then I felt appreciated and wanted. I did not know it was wrong, but I knew that I had to keep it a secret—and I never questioned it. I just knew we did not want the secret to be known. Even now, I am confused but I did not know any better, because it was done with kindness and by family. And I was so young when it started. I never felt or knew I needed to tell anyone. All that was love to me.

What was not love, was when I moved back to Burnaby into a hostile environment where I was yelled at, ridiculed, beaten, and made to feel like I had no worth. That was not love—and I knew it well.

As I grew older, I was still looking for love, but my vision of what was right and love was always blurred. If a boy put his hand on my thigh. I would allow it to stay there. I would allow it to slide up, and I would allow him to touch me because that is what I was taught to do. That is what I knew. And who knew, maybe this boy would turn into my Prince Charming. He would fall deeply and madly in love with me because I let him do what he wanted. I allowed him to be in control.

As time passed, the requests to do more than just touch increased. And again, it was not that I did not have self-respect for myself, because I did. I just did not have boundaries. I did not know that it was not my responsibility to give the man what he wanted. I lost that ability to understand what was right and wrong when it came to love and sex. All I wanted was to be loved. And if this was what was going to allow me to feel loved, even temporarily, then it was worth a shot. I needed to do it. I did not know any better. I had to do it.

Love. We do it all for love.

Now when I think of love, I think of self-care, self-respect, self-esteem, self-abundance, and self-everything. Sometimes I still find myself thinking about finding love, but now I know that I need to find that love for myself, and with myself, first and foremost before I can move forward with someone else.

After my Las Vegas romance, I did not think that I could love again. I felt like my true love had found me, and then left me to be in a marriage that he was not even happy to be in. I was broken, and it took me years to pick myself up and put the pieces back together.

Then I met my first boyfriend. Both of us were so damaged but trying to keep it concealed so that we could make the relationship work. Two damaged people trying to make ourselves better for each other seemed like it would be perfect because it involved self-love first and then mutual love. However, it was not like that.

Instead, we got into our vices, and we drank and got stuck in our own heads. We did not communicate properly, and we fought and yelled constantly—behaviours that we had learned and carried with us from our upbringings. We failed to do the self-care part and figured our traumas would work themselves out on their own. Eventually, our traumas manifested into despair, anger, rage, and hate. But somehow, we still stayed with each other, because at one point it was good and there was love—until there was not.

We stayed together for four years, on and off. Maybe only six months of our relationship were good. We eventually ended up outgrowing each other. I started working on myself and found self-love. But he never worked on himself. He thought that when he finally got the perfect job that things would miraculously fix themselves. But that perfect job never came, and we never fixed our relationship.

Instead, the love I gained for myself equalled to hating him to the point that my teeth would clench, my body would shake, and I would get stiff. There was so much anger within me. My body had been telling me for years that this was not working. Even sex became painful when that was the only thing that kept us together.

L.O.V.E.

Our relationship was well overdone—past expiration, should have never started, finally came to an end, or something we both needed to fill the void with. Even though he wanted to make it work, I could not. I needed to realize that I needed to stop putting myself into situations that just catered to the man—to make him happy, to be his trophy wife and his breadwinner. I was done and I needed to fix myself.

And that is love. Love fucks us up. It makes us think that some situations can work when 'love' is there. It makes us believe that happiness is around the corner—just wait it out. That is love.

No longer, will I cater to a man unless he is putting in the work, and loving me back. When he gives me that equal 50/50 then I am in and willing to try.

Chapter Ten

Who am I?

For a long time, I pondered the question of who am I? I have been through a lot in my life and for most of it, I kept moving through. How I did it sometimes, I have no idea. It took me a long time to realize who I even was.

I know I was always 'real', but I guess I never lived authentically. I did not go around telling people, 'Oh my god, you will not believe what happened to me as a child.' Instead, I would be 'real' in the moment and express how I felt—usually with a smile on my face because that is just who I am. A young woman with a whole assortment of masks, ready to pull one out for any situation. That was me, a true chameleon at its finest.

When I was working through my traumas, I noticed that I was saying things like, I am like this because of this—this is who I am. I am this way because this happened to me.

Yes, there is some importance to correlate the two with our pent-up emotions, ailments, and traumas. But these events do not define *who* you are. Who you are is defined by what you think about yourself. It is how you choose to get up in the morning and go about your day. It is how you choose to treat people—even when you are at your worst. Do you treat them with kindness, or do you lash out?

Our traumas do not define us. It is what we learn and take away from our traumas that define us. They become part of our story, but never the main character, just a sidekick. We go through our traumas because we are expected to learn something from them.

Unfortunately, many of us do not start to heal until we have dire situations happen to us and are forced to be alone with our thoughts—or even worse silence. Others do not even make it to that stage. Instead of working to overcome their traumas, they start using drugs, drinking, and participating in high-risk behaviours all to numb the pain, leading to other vicious cycles.

It is not fair who comes out and who does not. But ultimately, we all have a choice. If you choose to ignore your past, Spirit or the Universe will keep putting you into the same predicaments, until you are forced to deal with the situation and learn from it. If you do not, then welcome to your next birth cycle. Karma follows you, plus all the Karma you have accumulated in this birth—it all follows.

It is easy to look for ways out without having to deal with your past. Some of us find it through a needle, alcohol, sex, poor relationships, or other bad choices. It is easy to do, and sometimes it just feels better not having to deal with it all. Trust me I know. I used to drink a lot.

You would never see me out without at least a double in my hand and more on the way. Not to mention the strong beers I used to coat my stomach before I even touched the hard liquor. I think, at one point, I had gotten my tolerance up to four strong beers and fourteen doubles. I was self-medicating, and I did not even know I was.

That is the thing; sometimes we do not even know how much our traumas have affected us until it is too late. I had to get injured at work to realize that I needed to change.

After my 2015 injury, I continued to drink even more just to cope with the unknown/known traumas, and to deal with the pain in my body. It was not until my pain got so bad that I had to be off work that I would eventually shift from hard liquor to beer.

Still not correlating the two, I got injured again in 2016. This time, I went on an antidepressant to cope, and my life went mute. I could not feel the emotions that I was experiencing. Let alone trying to tell anyone what I was struggling with, because my serotonin levels were skyrocketing, and all I could do was smile. For the first time in my life, when I did not want to smile, I was forced to, and I hated myself for it.

I could not deal with my blunted emotions, and I eventually took myself off the medication—cold turkey. I know you are not supposed to stop like that, but at that point it was either me going clinically crazy, or me getting back to me. I chose the latter. It was one of the worst experiences of my life, and I will never go on an antidepressant again.

Liquor eventually became my main accomplice, my go-to, my liquid courage. I was invincible. People knew me and I knew people. I was coherent, fun, and always dancing center stage. But after my injury, I stopped going out and I secluded myself. I even stopped drinking for a while because I realized that my pain would get worse the day after.

Here is something that they do not advertise on a liquor bottle: *if you are experiencing any type of physical pain, alcohol will increase your inflammation the next day, causing you to be in more pain than the day before!* I would not cut out liquor completely until April 2021.

So, who am I now? Past the trauma, past the booze, past the negative beliefs that I gained from all of this. I am Mila Sharma. I am a SURVIVOR. I am POWERFUL. I am STRONG and BEAUTIFUL. I am a FIGHTER. I am a HEALER. I am COMPASSIONATE. I am the STRENGTH that I never knew I had.

No situation or person defines who I am as a person. I define who I am. And who I am, is a bad-ass rebel who found her voice and spoke her truth. I am LOVE and LIGHT.

Chapter Eleven
Anger (Part 1)

I was mad about a lot of things. I was mad that I was never allowed to speak about my experiences after moving back to Burnaby. I was mad that my dad always found a way to irritate me and treat me like shit. I was mad that my brother could not treat me like a sister—and often only made enough plates for four people; there were five of us. I was mad that I was constantly bullied by my entire family, treated like Cinderella, and never acknowledged. I was mad.

I always thought that the physical abuse was the worst because it hurt, and the emotional abuse was equally as bad because they both go hand in hand. Perhaps, I always thought it was the worst because no one ever hits someone they love. No one ever tells someone they are stupid in love.

It took me a long time to forgive my family for all the things they put me through, especially my dad, and my brother.

In Burnaby, I never had a safe haven in my home with my family. My room was only meant to be used to either study or sleep. Otherwise, I was expected to sit out in the living room, so that everyone knew where I was.

At one point my dad had even removed the door from my bedroom so that I would stop slamming it out of frustration. I was a teenager. Even when my door would be closed, no one ever knocked to see if they could come in or not. They just barged in to see what I was up to, or to tell me to go sit outside.

The few moments I had to myself were never mine. I never had a chance to decompress and let my emotions out. Instead, I would have to go to the bathroom and lock the door, so that I could cry in silence.

As much as my dad complained about his treatment by his father growing up, he did the same to me. Despite what he proclaimed out loud that he loves all his children the same, there was a clear difference in how he treated me compared to my brother, and my sister.

Perhaps, he was taking out his frustrations on me because he hated parts of himself, and

ANGER (PART 1)

I reminded him of himself. A black sheep recognizing another black sheep. The beatings to the verbal put-downs made me hate myself.

How could someone be so mean? How could someone treat a child like that? If you hated your childhood so much, then why did you not try harder to change the mould? Why did you continue to live in your power and treat me like you did?

My brother had the privilege of being the victim of the physical and mental abuse inflicted by our dad until it eventually became my title to hold. Despite understanding what it felt like to be on the receiving end of the abuse, he continued to follow in the steps of our dad with me.

Reflecting on the past, I understand why he may have thought I deserved the abuse. As a victim, you typically only think that you are the only one who has gone through it. His frustrations with the situation came out on me because I had lived in Prince George, and he presumably thought I left that household unscathed.

I suppose it was a safe assumption because I remained close with my Prince George family, while he distanced himself from them with good reason. Little did he know that I had gone through the same sexual abuse as he had, if not longer and more frequently.

All I needed was support when I moved to Burnaby with my family. And I did not receive it from anyone other than my Prince George family. They were the only ones, at the time, who I felt understood my pain. I know the influence and control that my Prince George family had over me, made my relationship with my own family more strained. But I was just a child who needed to be loved. I needed to feel safe and supported.

Even though no one in my family knew about the sexual abuse I went through—it never changed me from treating anyone less than they deserved. But maybe it was because I was just a small girl with no authority. I was taught to be weaker than the man. Not just physically but mentally as well. I became passive and my light dimmed lower and lower. The times I did try to resist, I was put back into my place with unnecessary force.

No matter how much I cried to my mom about what was happening, she never wanted to hear it. As soon as I would mention the names of my dad or my brother, she would get extremely mad. Suddenly, I would be placed at fault as if I was the one causing the trouble, even though I was not.

In her eyes and her upbringing, the man could do no wrong. The man was to be praised, respected, and treated like he was God. The man was our

ANGER (PART 1)

provider. It never occurred to her that she was providing for us too.

When I was born, my mom was working three jobs to support our family while our dad was looking for work. She supported us. She provided. She was doing what a man was supposed to do.

As for my sister, she was always overprotective and cynical of the world. She never let me make my own friends or liked anyone I made friends with. I became dependent on her and what she wanted me to be. At times, I would rebel against her and my family, but I was always weaker, and they all reminded me of that.

I lost myself trying to cater to my family, and I tried hard to be who they expected me to be. As a girl, I was taught to put my own needs last, because what I had learned was that I was not a priority. And eventually, I started to treat everyone I met as a priority and ignored myself.

These suppressed emotions and feelings caused me to accumulate so much anger towards my family. I was not able to speak about my struggles or what I needed to make my transition easier. All I knew was that I was always in the wrong and they knew best.

The more I tried to suppress my anger, the more it grew. I needed to find the balance between my anger and my emotions. I had to put in a lot of effort to get better so that I could rid myself of this anger. I learned Reiki and tried meditating, all the many things to try to calm my mind, but it was not working. First off, I was living at home and constantly had my 'fight and flight' responses in continual overdrive.

Until eventually, I could not take it anymore. My dad pulled the last straw and in 2019, I moved out. No more waiting for my Prince Charming or my boyfriend to finally get his life together. I moved.

And to think even before I signed the papers to move, my dad told me that I was making a big mistake and that I was going to regret it. The funny thing is, it was the best decision that I had made in my life because for once, I was doing something for myself.

You cannot change the past, but you can change what is happening in the present.

You need to understand that you cannot change anyone. The only person that you have the power to change is yourself. You control your emotions, and you control how you react to situations. So, start making yourself a priority and start loving yourself, even if that means you need to leave people or situations behind.

Chapter Twelve

Forgiveness

You may think that I stayed way too long with my parents, but it was all I knew. Even though I dreamt of moving out many times, I always assumed that it would be with my Prince Charming. The traditional way for an Indian girl to move out of her family home.

I stayed for two reasons.

The first reason was that I did not think I could make it out in the world on my own.

The second reason was because of my mom. I stayed to support her. Regardless, of how blinded she was when it came to her love for my dad, and my brother. I stayed for her.

With time, I eventually realized that I needed to stop living her life and start living my own. Had my dad not pushed me to my limit, I might still be living with them. But that day, something inside me told me 'enough.' And in 2019, I moved out to start my journey of healing.

As much as I love my family, they did not allow me to grow and experience life as I should have. I partied and drank like most young adults did, but I did not experience things that people my age already had. I was a late bloomer in life. And the alcohol I drank, masked most of my emotions. Emotions that I should have dealt with earlier, but either I did not know I could, or I refused to acknowledge them. It was not until my 2015 work injury that stopped me, and it still took me four more years to really address my past traumas in detail.

Forgiveness was not easy for me, as I am sure most people who have had to forgive others know that. But forgiveness is tangible, and it is necessary to forgive yourself and others so that you can truly heal.

It took me moving out of the house to start my journey of forgiveness for my family. Once I removed myself from the constant battle of having my 'fight and flight' responses elevated, I could calm my mind and body, and look at the situation from the outside in.

Working on myself led me to know just how many internal conflicts I was holding onto. It also allowed me to see how capable and strong I was for dealing with all I had dealt with. I gained the confidence I needed to move forward. It was during this time that I met Baby Mila through my self-help books and counselling sessions.

Ultimately, you begin to realize that most of the traumas that have occurred in your life have been because of unresolved traumas of the person who is causing them in your life.

Inevitably, how I was being treated at home was how I was treating my then-boyfriend. I used him to take out my anger. And no matter how many times I told him that this was not working and that he needed to find someone who treated him better, he still stayed. In his own household, he grew up with this, so in a sense, history was repeating itself. Except he took the role of his mother, and I took the one of his father.

By removing myself from these situations, I was able to reflect on my learned behaviours. I was able to see that I was living the life I never wished to live. It was part of my own reflections that forced me to make even more changes within myself to be better to myself and others.

I was also able to recognize the hardships that happened to my family that caused them to behave and become the people they became. As a result, it became evident that they were just trying to cope as best as they knew how from what they learned and experienced in their own lives.

It was this recognition that allowed me to forgive myself because the way that they were treating me was a direct reflection of what they thought about themselves. It then made it easier for me to forgive them because they were just people trying to get through their day. I am not saying what they put me through was right, but it gave me a new perspective on how I choose not to be.

I now understand the quietness and power of my own strength. You do not have to yell or shout to be powerful to show your strength. Some of the strongest people lead in silence and persevere through their internal battles. And I am so grateful to be one of those people who overcame and conquered that depth of forgiveness.

There is light at the end of the tunnel. Find a safe place and reflect. Remove your emotions and look at your situation from the lens of yourself as well as your abuser. What do you see? What are the lessons you have learned from this, or are still learning? Now empower yourself with this newfound information. And be the strength that you need to be, in order to move away from being a victim to a true survivor!

Chapter Thirteen

Consequences

What happens when you do not speak the truth about your trauma? It can manifest in various aspects of your life—in relationships, in situations, and in everyday life. Mine manifested in several ways, notably in poor relationships both intimately and in health. It seemed that the people who I was attracting into my life were only nice because they wanted something. Then, after taking advantage of my kindness, they would leave without reciprocating. I never had loyal or long-term friends. When people entered my life, I would try to analyze them before they could hurt me. Unfortunately, I would remain naïve, thinking that all people were good until they were not. I was always too trusting.

My car—eager to drive, I bought myself a 2015 Mini Cooper. It was the only car I wanted, and the only one that fit my personality. I was sold on it, the moment I saw it. But slowly, one by one, bad things kept happening. The windshield wipers made rubbing sounds and the trunk leaked water. I popped a tire on a nail driving down the highway—it seemed unavoidable at the time. Then I bent my rim by going down a hill too fast and hitting a pothole. My rim and tire have never been the same. All that happened within the first year and a half. After that, I was driving down the highway with my sister and our puppy, and a rock the size of a golf ball came flying at us and cracked my entire windshield. At this point, I had no idea that all these issues that I was experiencing were even remotely linked to me not dealing with my past.

As for my health. Trauma creeps up in so many ways. It might start with our material possessions, then it can manifest either physically, mentally, or both. It can start with a small pain in your body that spreads. Or worse, it can turn into lumps or bumps that can eventually turn into something malignant.

My trauma started with body pain. First, my ankles and my hips hurt, leading to tension elsewhere. When I had my 2015 injury, the pain started in my back, neck, and shoulders, and eventually crept throughout my entire body, causing fibromyalgia and edema in my lower legs. No medical tests or doctors could figure out how a soft tissue injury could manifest into all this. At twenty-eight years old, I was officially diagnosed with chronic pain.

At that point, I became scared to live. I was going for massages, physiotherapy, and acupuncture at least three to five times a week. My full-time job of nursing now became a full-time job of taking myself to appointments and trying to nurse myself back to life. I was too far gone. Any false move could put me in pain.

Walking too long put me in pain. Sitting put me in pain. Moving put me in pain. At that point, medications were not even working. I became immune to Ibuprofen, a miracle drug that I could no longer take because it was putting my body through too much stress with my kidneys and creating water retention all down my legs. I tried to stay positive, but I was losing it mentally.

All my life, I had tried to be good, even after enduring such a difficult upbringing. With my patients, I was known for putting them first before myself. I gave kisses to the little old ladies and made love out of nothing in every situation. I was a ray of sunshine, always the girl who looked too good to be at work with my colourful personality, pink lips, and bright scrubs. That was me. And now that part of me was becoming angry, cynical, hateful, and cold—all because I was constantly in pain.

For a long time, I denied having any mental health issues when speaking with my doctors or anyone else. I figured that if I was not diagnosed with it then I did not have it. But the fact was, I was struggling, and no one knew. At the time, I thought my physical pain was only due to my injury, but it was not.

In 2017, I was officially diagnosed with depression, anxiety, and post-traumatic stress disorder—still related to work, I never told anyone about the abuse I had gone through. I did not think it was relevant nor had anything to do with this. And maybe it did not, and that is why I could not shake this.

Then in 2018, I developed excessively red and dry eyes. I saw my doctor and instead of prescribing me allergy eye drops, she referred me to an ophthalmologist. They discovered that I had developed a multitude of macular holes in the retinas of both of my eyes. If not treated, it could impede my ability to see. Still not correlating the stress of my past with the ailments of the present, I continued to develop more holes in my left eye, even after having surgery. I tried asking my ophthalmologist and surgeon about the cause of these holes, but no one was able to give me a concrete answer. Finally, one suggested that it was my allergies that were attacking my eyes and causing the holes. I still do not know how much of that I believed.

It was not until I met with my Reiki master, who told me that there was something I was not seeing and that there was something I needed to deal with. The only traumas I thought I needed to heal from were the physical and mental abuses—nothing else seemed bad at the time.

That is why it is so important to listen to your body and to pay attention to signs of stress. Your body is trying to guide you and open your eyes to things that need fixing. If not, it will come in various forms. And the last thing you want is it to reach a state of no return. What happens if it turns into stage IV liver cancer?

Chapter Fourteen

Truth

My truth or their truth? Who are they going to believe? I am just a small girl who does not know any better. Do I speak about what happened or do I stay silent?

Sometimes, when I look back at who I told at the ages of thirty-one, thirty-two, and thirty-four—it seems surreal. How difficult it was to speak my truth at each age. At thirty-one, I was still in shock and just tucked it away. At thirty-two, it was painful telling my sister, my other half, but I needed it to be out for her to heal. And again, I thought that I had dealt with it, but I guess I had placed it aside.

When my eyes began to get worse, I knew there was still something that I was not seeing. All these years, the one abuse that I thought was the least bad, was the one that my body was hurting from the most.

Then, on March 14th, 2021, my grandfather passed away. We drove up to Prince George on March 13th at 22:00, after receiving a call from my Prince George dad informing us of our grandfather's condition. We did not get there until the next morning at 07:00. Afraid to go directly to the house, I made a detour to the university while my mom and sister slept, so that I could catch my breath. I had not been back to Prince George for over seven years, and even though the town was the same, I felt overwhelmed, but at home.

We walked into the house and were greeted by my Prince George parents. My grandfather had passed away hours earlier, but no one had wanted to call us for fear that we would turn around and go back home. Our twenty-four-hour visit ended up being seven days of reminiscing, tears, liquor, forgiveness, and the resurfacing of a trauma that I did not know still affected me.

Everyone greeted us with love, almost as if there had never been a break, despite this being the same family who had refused to provide my parents, and my brother with the justice that they had so needed seven years prior. My older cousins were married with children. All three cousins were there: the two sisters and brother—the perpetrator of my sexual abuse. My female cousins had their own children: a newborn and the others two and eight years old. My male cousin had come with his two kids, aged five and eight. His wife had decided to stay home and work, also, to probably avoid family politics.

We were there together, acting as if there had been no breaks or issues between us. It felt good to be with my cousins again. All their children were so pure, so innocent, so sweet. It stirred up a lot of emotions for me, more than I had anticipated.

Eventually, when it was just us girls (my sister and my female cousins), we finally spoke about the past, and how good it felt to be reunited. We spoke up on how things had been handled, and our lives in the past seven years. It was heated, and it was tearful. Their traumas were always worse than anyone else's, which we have had to swallow our pride for. But out of all of us, myself being the youngest, it was my health that was deteriorating the most. My body was hurting, and I had developed another macular hole in my eye that required another appointment with the surgeon.

Being around everyone, I did not know if we were drinking to celebrate our grandfather's life or being together. But I was constantly drinking. I was drinking to get my creative juices flowing to paint my grandfather's mural. I was drinking for breakfast. I was drinking like I was on vacation, but I was not. I was drinking to cope. I would not realize this until I was later able to self-reflect in the safety of my own home. And their kids, even though it was not their fault, they brought up my emotions of lost time and how I had been that age once. It also brought my emotions out about how my innocence was lost at the hands of the father of two of the kids. I drank to keep my emotions down. I drank to stay happy. I drank to deal with my childhood memories.

Two main triggers happened to me when I was in Prince George. It was not from being in the house or going into the rooms where the sexual abuse used to happen. It was not even from being around my male cousin, because I had swallowed what had happened to me for years, and like I said, it just did not affect me like it should have.

The first trigger happened when I offered to put his daughter to bed. I carried her up the stairs to my grandfather's room where they were staying. Because she felt warm to me and I did not want her to be uncomfortable, I decided to take off her pants. As I was taking off her pants, her underwear came down a bit from the sides, and while still asleep, her reflexes quickly pulled them up. I left her shirt and underwear on and tucked her into bed. That knee-jerk reaction of her pulling up her underwear like that brought up my childhood. Was he doing this to his own daughter too? Am I going crazy? Was this a natural instinct for a child to instinctively pull up their underwear while still being asleep?

I headed back downstairs. I told him that I had put her to bed and took off her pants so she would not get too hot. All he said was, 'Okay, thanks.' And I went to get myself another drink.

The second trigger happened the night before we were going to leave. That night, I was drinking wine. I never drink wine, but I was—red out of everything. We were all having a good time. His daughter got tired, and he said he was going to put her to bed and then come back down. We waited but he never came back. So, I offered to go up and get him. I do not know how many glasses I had had at this point, but I still felt coherent and functional. I gently knocked on the door and opened it.

He was laying with his arms wrapped around her. To someone who was not molested for seven years, maybe this would appear innocent. To me, it reminded me of my childhood. This is how he used to hold me, and I wanted to cry, to scream, to yell, but something held me back.

He snarled at me, and I asked him if he was coming down and left. That image stuck with me. I was stuck with that image. And again, those thoughts flooded my mind. Is this happening to her? Is her innocence being robbed, or is she special, and does not deserve to be touched like I was? I then helped myself to another several glasses to swallow my emotional pain.

Coming back home, I met with my counsellor and asked what I should do. Do I need to tell someone, a.k.a. his sisters? And it came back to 'What does your heart tell you to do?' Frustrated with her question, I stopped seeing her after that appointment. Ultimately though, she was right. I had been ignoring my own needs and emotions for so long. What did my heart want me to do? Better yet, what did my heart need me to do?

A few weeks later, my sister and I drove to Prince George despite the dismay of our parents, as they thought it was disrespectful to our brother. However, considering we were not on speaking terms with him because he did not feel like we were being supportive of his trauma, we went ahead with our trip. A trip that I desperately needed to go on.

My male cousin and his kids had left to go home and were no longer in Prince George. Surprisingly, this visit would go much differently than the last. Our grandfather was gone, and everyone seemed to be more relaxed. I hardly drank, which I think surprised everyone. I was always the muchie (fish) and ready for a drink! Instead, I took this trip as a healing retreat. Through my oldest female cousin, I was introduced to a lady who would later become my mentor and help me with my journey of self-recovery.

Prior to the trip, I tried figuring out if I should tell my female cousins about my sexual abuse or not. I did not. I kept my secret to myself and thought that if I continued my healing journey, then they would never have to know. I would be healed on my own!

In mid-April 2021, I stopped drinking. I no longer wanted to be a victim, and I wanted to face my trauma head-on instead of drinking it away. I needed to be brave and do it. So, I did.

Chapter Fifteen

Reflections

After my trip to Prince George, I came home, and I could not stop thinking about their kids. This time, I had had a chance to see and play with the youngest female cousin's two-year-old daughter. How many times had I been left alone with her, where anything could have happened? Not that I had any intention, because I would never wish what happened to me on anyone else. But how easy it is to build trust in a family where no one will ever suspect the worst.

Two years old was the earliest time that I can recall the sexual abuse starting. I secluded myself from both my families (biological and Prince George). I wanted to be alone. I needed time to mourn my childhood, and the trauma I had endured. I needed to forgive myself. I needed to recognize that it was not my fault. I needed to forgive my male cousin for the sexual abuse he inflicted on me. I needed to remember that I had no control over what had happened. I had been younger, smaller, and naïve, and he had taken advantage of that. I needed to forgive myself, my male cousin, and the situation so that I could heal.

It was almost as if, when my grandfather passed away, all the walls and locked doors suddenly disappeared. It was like an awakening; everything needed to be brought to light. No more protecting anyone. Now that he was gone, I felt like his spirit knew the truth, and was giving me the permission, I needed to share the trauma.

I continued to work with my mentor, and she performed a treatment for me called, the Black Pearl Technique, which shrinks the trauma portion of your brain and minimizes your 'fight and flight' responses. Even though the treatments were done remotely, it was uncomfortable, to say the least. I could feel the warmth of her hands on my head, but I was never relaxed. I dreaded our appointments together, but I knew that if I did not go through with them then I would not be able to heal as fast as I wanted to. And believe me, I had been working on myself for several years and I was getting tired and frustrated as to why I was not healing.

I remember feeling nauseous and experiencing bouts of vertigo weeks after the treatments.

However, there was no other way to explain it other than the shifts of energy within my psyche. Although bad, it was nowhere close to how I had felt when I was going off the antidepressant cold turkey. This was more than doable. I could push through. Eventually, my plan to keep my secret failed me. I think the more treatments I underwent, the more my body grieved and enabled me to unveil this dark and horrible hidden truth.

In May 2021, I was completely inconsolable. I could not stop crying, and I was so anxious. I knew my secret needed to be shared. One Saturday night, I decided to call the youngest female cousin of the two. Conveniently, both sisters were together. Initially, I could not find the words, but they heard my cries, and they heard my pain. Finally, I was able to mutter out the words, 'Your brother did the same thing to me that he did to my brother.'

There was silence. There was shock. There were tears. My oldest female cousin wanted to know what my mentor had said about it. Not what I needed to hear when I had just confessed my biggest, deepest, and darkest secret—almost as if I was lying. Once again, I became angry.

The moment that I told my female cousins, things became surreal. I went to bed that night and I could not remember if what I had done was a dream or real life. I felt like I had too much to drink and blacked out, but the truth was that I was more than sober. It was my emotions that had become painfully heightened that I could not tell.

It took me a few days to realize and process the events. But my female cousins seemed supportive and checked in with me and thanked me for being brave enough to share my truth. Quite honestly, I did not know how I was going to tell them or how they would take the information. I just remember feeling so broken that I needed to make the phone call. When I called, they accepted my trauma.

In the end, though, their main concern was how to protect their parents (my Prince George parents). But what about my parents? They had suffered for over seven years trying to seek justice for what had happened to their son, my brother. And I was damn sure that I did not want to put them in the same situation. My parents finally seemed to be in a somewhat decent state, and I did not want to sabotage or rob them of whatever happiness they had left.

This entire time, I had held onto this secret. And after telling my female cousins, I felt so light. I did not feel like my body hurt as much, and my mind felt clearer. But within time, the pain crept back, and I developed another macular hole in my eye.

Chapter Sixteen

Burden

All my life, this has been my burden to hold, but it should not have been a burden at all. If we had the insight or power to control a situation when we were first placed into it, the likelihood of us saying 'No' would have been a high priority. Unfortunately, we are not given that insight. So, instead, we have to go through these experiences in hopes of finding light at the end of the tunnel, and eventually the truth of the matter.

No one tells you how painful or long this journey is. And no one tells you that when you start this journey, there are bound to be negative emotions or feelings that come up. And much like a drug addict, we can experience relapses. It is definitely not a walk in the park. The journey is a long, treacherous one that you can either face on your own or ask for help.

Even though I had a few key support people who guided me along, I did my journey on my own.

People that I needed came into my life and gave me the tools that I needed to broaden my insight. However, none of them knew the extent of my trauma. I did not think that it was relevant to share it with them at the time, nor did I know the extent of the trauma that I was dealing with.

Sometimes, the conversations that we have to have with someone about our situation can be difficult. Not only for yourself for sharing it, but for the person who is listening. You never know how they are going to react or process the information. But that is the chance we take when we share our journey. And the more we share our journey, the easier it is to talk about it. Often, you will wake up and amaze yourself in regards to how far you have come, or find that you have released yourself because you spoke your truth.

These abuses should not be burdens. And we should not be afraid to speak up to make someone else feel less uncomfortable. Everyone needs to know that these things happen. But the saddest part of all of this is that they do not. Victims are afraid to speak up. Sometimes, it is just easier to swallow it or tuck it away for another day or another lifetime.

I held onto my burden for thirty-four years until I finally found a release. And even after I told my female cousins, I felt a sense of sadness because the burden that I had held onto for so long to protect everyone was now theirs. Even though they assured me that it was not a burden, I felt like it was.

One of the questions that they asked me was, 'What do you feel that needs to be done?' I had not even thought that far. My concern was telling them about what had happened and that was it. Frankly, it is the aftermath that will have the biggest impact compared to when we let our secret out of the bag.

So, what did I want? Did I want a resolution? Did I want him to know? Did I want him to be held accountable? Did I want an apology?

First thing first, you need to realize that an apology is not always something that you are going to get or need in order to heal. Also, do you want to force an apology if it is not genuine? Should not the apology be sincere, and the other party be actually sorry for their actions?

At the time, all I wanted was for them to listen to my story, and I had had that. I gave them the option to ask him about it for their own healing. But I was adamant that I did not want to talk to him or hear what he had to say. Sometimes, there are reasons as to why people do the things they do. Like, did it happen to them in the past, or is it just the person they are?

Weeks went by and they had still not spoken to him. Was I not a concern or did they just not know what to say? After all, it was a huge secret that I had told them, so part of me understood that. And since I was still under the mentality that this was my burden, I felt like I should take it into my own hands. So, on the full moon of June 2021, the time when one surrenders all of what they no longer need, I messaged him.

I said, 'I told your sisters what happened. And I do not expect a message back, but I forgive you.' I never received a response. Instead, I was blocked.

On June 24th, 2021, I finally felt free.

Chapter Seventeen

Therapies

Counselling. Some people swear by this, for me, I am still on the fence. However, for someone who loves to talk, then maybe this could be for you. I am not a talker, nor do I like to open up about myself if I do not have to. With that being said, counselling did get me out of my comfort zone.

Before starting, you might want to shop around for a counsellor or psychologist. Find someone who understands your cultural background because not every culture will understand the dynamics.

Counselling forced me to start talking out loud about my traumas. The first trauma that I worked on was the sexual abuse I endured from my male cousin. Truthfully, I was done dealing with it after one session. Like I said, it did not knowingly affect me until I met my cousins' children.

My second trauma was about my experience moving from Prince George to Burnaby. There was one situation where I had a round brush stuck in my hair, and I was called downstairs to eat by my dad. From what I can recall, I said 'No'. I remember him charging up the stairs and dragging me by my hair to go eat. It was only after that that he realized that there was a comb stuck in my hair. Later, he helped take it out.

My third trauma had to do with getting into a fight with my brother, and I was crying. I remember my dad coming inside the house holding a car rim asking, 'Who is crying?' My brother pointed to me, and just like that, I got hit right in the face with the rim and was told to stop crying.

Those sessions took time and a lot of work. Speaking and building a rapport with my inner child while doing a treatment called Eye Movement Desensitization and Reprocessing Therapy (EMDR). The best way to describe EMDR is by visualizing a snapshot of one of your worst memories. The counsellor or psychologist then waves their hand in the air from side to side. As you follow their hand movements with your eyes, you continue to visualize this picture. Sometimes, you might experience tingling on your head, pain in your body, emotions, or nothing at all. You continue this process as many times as needed. Each time you visualize this picture, you will slowly see how the image softens. Eventually, you become less triggered by the trauma and the emotions attached to it.

I slowly worked to exchange those snapshots and memories of me getting physically abused with prettier memories. I would change the comb in my hair to flowers and would fill up the entire mental canvas with red roses until all I could see were me and the roses.

I then worked on removing the baby version of myself from the house. I had to talk to myself and build trust to take Baby Mila away. And when I took her out of the house, we floated away in a red air balloon, far into the sky, and into the abyss where she could no longer be persecuted or abused.

With counselling, you have to be open to questions like 'What are you thinking right now?' or 'How does that make you feel?' As frustrating as those questions are, sometimes you might be surprised with your answers.

Journaling. YELL AS LOUDLY AS YOU WANT to yourself through paper. There is something therapeutic when it comes to taking a pen or pencil, putting it against the paper, and letting whatever is stuck inside your mind come out. I journaled a lot. I journaled until my hand cramped up or until I ran out of ink. I journaled until my papers were soaked from all the tears falling from my eyes. I journaled. It was my emotional release. My safe zone. No one could tell me that I was wrong in my journal. Instead, I could tell myself what I was worth, and what was on my mind.

I have done a lot using journaling. I have written letters to ex-loves, my abusers, my mom, and myself, and burned them all. With the flames, I would then let the smoke be released into the universe, only to have it returned with love. My letters were often about how they made me feel and the forgiveness that I gave to myself and them.

Quite honestly, you might need to write a few letters to get to the healing stage that you are looking for. You might be so angry that literally, every other word you write is a F-Bomb! And you can feel that tension flowing from your head to your clenched jaw and your tight muscles, and feel the intensity of the ink on the paper. Your writing will often reflect your emotions. Eventually, when you write enough times, and you do the work to accept what has happened. Things will eventually lead to forgiveness.

The hardest letter I ever had to write was one to myself. I found that I have had to write a few letters to myself at different stages of my healing processes. But finding self-acceptance and love for yourself can be a task. Especially when you have to forgive and apologize to a younger version of yourself, and to constantly have to remind yourself that it was not your fault and that what happened does not define you now. Only then will you notice a shift in your healing process.

It is easy to complain on paper, but eventually, you need to find appreciation for yourself. Most times, we are so fixated on those who have caused us pain that we neglect our own needs. We need to truly love ourselves before we can really heal. So, do not expect overnight success. This is hard and it will only get worse before it gets better. But trust that—it does get better.

Chapter Eighteen
Sabotage

It is easy to fall victim to self-sabotage. Just when everything seems to be making sense in life and falling into place, here comes ourselves and we sabotage ourselves all over again.

This can be self-sabotage of our self-worth, our relationships, or our healing. Sometimes, it is caused because we do not have enough self-love, to begin with. Other times, it is because we do not have our boundaries set, or we have not worked on ourselves enough to figure out what our fears or anxieties are.

I self-sabotaged my healing many times. When I hit a rough patch, instead of facing it head-on or dealing with the emotions, I would hit the bottle. A few drinks later and I would forget what I was even upset about. I would go back to being a happy drinker. It was very seldom that I would drink to deal with my emotions, it was more common to drink them away.

In a recent relationship, one that I was sober for—my self-sabotage got the best of me. It was the perfect date, followed by a second, equally passionate one. Instead of flowing with the energy and his vibe, I tried to control the situation. I had made a promise to myself a long time ago that I would never let a man control the situation. I guess, three male traumas later, I was good with my promise.

Instead, I was forcing the narrative of what he thought about me, or when we could meet next. I never heard from him after that. Even during our first date, I was already wanting to tell him about my traumas so that I could avoid the self-sabotaging later, and that way he would understand my emotional issues. Ultimately, I had wanted him to know why I was the way I was.

But I guess that was the problem. I was the way I was because of those nasty traumas and not the other way around. Instead, it was those experiences that shaped me into the woman that I am today. I did not turn into the woman I am because of those. My thinking was crossed.

To add, I would not even let him hug me until I was ready and prepared for it. The Baby Mila part of me felt that if I let him initiate a hug, then I would be giving him the power to crush me. I was not ready to give up my control, so I did not let him. Even our first kiss, I initiated it, because if I started it then it would be on my terms and not his.

He was the first man that I would be with after coming to terms with my earliest trauma. Little did I know that this last little bit of my trauma that I was telling him that I was about to close, would be ripped back open when he left.

Chapter Nineteen
Working with Baby Mila

It took me a long time to start getting comfortable when talking to my baby self, Baby Mila. I felt weird talking to her. I was grown and I am Mila. Baby Mila grew up and became me, so why did I need to talk to her? It turns out that we all have smaller versions of ourselves inside of us, and they typically stop getting older when trauma first ensues. Baby Mila stopped growing at two years old. And in reality, so did my current age, when it came to creating relationships and boundaries. I did not have any.

I did a lot of mirrorwork to try to connect to Baby Mila. I wrote her letters. I cried. I held her tight in my mind and imagination. She needed to be cared for and loved. The truth was, so did I. I needed the same love and care that I was finally giving to her and, in return, giving to myself.

My biggest self-realization working with Baby Mila was how small and young she was. How vibrant her energy once was and how dim her light had turned when I had to find her. She was not the same little girl that I imagined her to be. I guess, during all those years of abuse, she got neglected while everyone else grew up, including myself.

Often, I would find my anxiety heighten because of something that had happened to Baby Mila, and she would experience the same anxiety. It was now my job to figure out the cause of it and to protect her. I always thought my biggest triumph had been getting her out of her Burnaby home and taking her away to a safer place. Oh, how the anxiety passed, and I felt that much better. Finally, I could sleep with ease because Baby Mila was safe. Baby Mila was finally free.

Or so I thought...

After my break with this new man, I never received the closure that I needed. I felt abandoned and my entire childhood came back to me. I had never thought that I could fall that low again until that happened. One more feeling that needed major attention, one I never knew I needed to attend to because I had finally felt at home. I was living in my new townhouse, no longer living between two homes and two families. I was free until that moment.

I felt like I hit rock bottom. I cried like I had not cried in a long time. I got into a car accident. I got a parking ticket. I developed another macular hole in my eye that required immediate surgery. My life crumbled and I felt unworthy and not good enough. Not once in my life have I felt my confidence fall that low. I was done and I did not think that I would ever find myself again. To top it off, that anxiety that I had felt years ago came back in full swing.

Baby Mila was back and with an issue that we both did not know was a concern until that moment. That feeling of abandonment that was causing the anxiety was because we had freed Baby Mila from her family home in Burnaby, but we left her in Prince George. Baby Mila was abandoned and forgotten about. So, once again I had to close my eyes and imagine freeing Baby Mila from the house.

With tears flowing down my face, I entered the house and I walked up the stairs to the room where the sexual abuse all began: my male cousin's childhood room that would later turn into mine. Baby Mila was sitting there alone on his bed in just her white underwear. Nothing more. I found her clothes and I helped her put them on. I explained to her that she was safe and that she was never going to have to come back here again. I picked up my two-year-old self and carried her out of the Prince George house to my townhouse, where she would stay with me forever—safe and close.

Anytime you feel angry, sad, or anxious about a situation, reflect to see if there was something in your past that is causing this stir of emotions in you. Then imagine yourself going back in time and freeing your small self from the negative situation. Make sure that you make yourself feel loved and safe and try not to put them back into the same or similar situation. Otherwise, the emotions will continue to manifest themselves in reality.

Chapter Twenty

Courage

Sometimes, you need to listen to that small voice in your head, the one that is telling you to face your fears and to be bold. It is that small bout of courage that will allow you to open up and start the process of healing. Ultimately though, it is up to you whether or not you are willing to listen.

When you start to listen to that small voice, eventually it will get bigger, and it will then be known as your intuition. The more you listen to your intuition, the more you will realize that this voice that you have been listening to, has been your Spirit Guides the entire time.

Each time we are born, we are given a task to experience and learn from in our human form. However, once we are born, we forget this conversation that we have had with Spirit or the Universe. It then becomes up to us to live our lives and try to figure out what our life purpose is, given the experiences that we are tasked with, no matter how loving or ugly they are. They help us experience what we need to in this lifetime so that we can complete our cycle.

Then, depending on what you believe in, we are either reincarnated into a different life form to experience something new, or we come back into human form to either complete a new task or the same task that we did not complete in our last life. If we are not reincarnated again because we completed our life lesson, then we can become Spirit Guides to someone else who chooses life in human form.

Our Spirit Guides choose us based on what we experience and things we need to work on. Some are with us from the time that we are conceived, while others come when we need them to, depending on what we need help with. Our Spirit Guides choose us. Sometimes, we do not even know that they are even there or that they exist.

So, every time that you think that you are having to experience the world alone, know that you are not. Your Spirit Guides are always with you, whispering in your ear. It is up to you to quiet yourself enough to listen.

Chapter Twenty-one
Letting go

Breathe in and breathe out. If only it was that easy to let go of trauma or learned behaviour. There is no exact timeframe that you can give yourself on when you want to let go of something.

Your first step in healing is to acknowledge what happened to you. You might cry. You might feel ashamed. You might feel an intense bout of fear, guilt, or anger. No emotion is a wrong emotion. Remember that we are all different and that we all experience our trauma differently. Therefore, the same process will not work for everyone.

You just need to be aware of your emotions and embrace them as your own. Because for once, this is something that you own, the trauma you do not. The trauma was an experience that you needed to go through in order to grow and heal from.

I am not going to go through the steps and processes of the emotions you are supposed to feel, because I believe that this should be a fluid approach and simple, much like breathing. So why can we not release our emotions the same way?

All I know is that the process cannot be rushed. It is dependent on you. Things are going to come up along the way as you start your journey that you did not even remember or know. And you will likely experience some setbacks that will cause you to go back to the initial feeling you had. Perhaps that emotion could not be cleared because you needed to remember or experience something else first before you could clear it.

I tried everything to let go of as much as I could as fast as I could. I journaled. I wrote letters. I burned and released them into the Universe. I expected to feel better, and initially, I did. However, the emotions kept creeping back. As I continued to start listening and opening myself up to Spirit and the Universe, I realized there were still situations that I had either not forgiven myself for or came across. Like I said, it is a process.

So, I journaled some more. I did Reiki on myself. I learned how to meditate, though I always found it hard to clear my mind enough to focus. But the point is, I kept trying. I did counselling. I shouted out obscenities into my pillow. I sang at the top of my lungs. I drove around to clear my head. I forced myself to walk outside even though it was not my favourite thing to do on my own. So, I did small tasks to get myself out, like phone a friend on route or take a detour to check the mail. Whatever it is, force yourself out of your comfort zone, no matter how much you dislike it. I also learned to dance again.

Before my 2015 injury, I was the 'greatest dancer alive'! *Hey, if you believe it then you absolutely are!* When I got injured, I let my life stop. I stopped living, and I stopped going out and dancing. So, to have to relearn how to dance proved itself quite difficult. I was off-balance. I was tripping over my own feet. I felt like I had no rhythm. And trust me, for those of you who have rhythm, you know when you have lost it. It took me a few years to get my footwork back in tune with my mind, but it was all in the process of letting go. Once I learned to let go, my body and mind were not as consumed with holding onto every single injury, memory, or emotion. I finally remembered what it felt like to be alive and present. My body finally felt free.

So, my words of advice, when you feel like you are going back a few steps rather than forward, do not get discouraged. Remember, you can do this! Just choose a few methods that worked for you in the past to help release emotions and try to do it again. And if that is not working, then find something else. Try having a bath or sitting by the ocean. When you start letting go, you will start attracting new things into your life. You will start learning things that you did not know you needed to know.

For example, I hated baths. I felt trapped whenever I was in one. And for someone who cannot sit in one place for long, because it is not something you are used to, it can be challenging. But it taught me that I needed to stop and start loving myself. It also taught me that I needed to be patient with myself. It forced me to re-evaluate things in my life and to see what was important. And just as the water flows down the drain—you let it all go.

Chapter Twenty-two

My fear of men

My fears probably stem from three male-run traumas and a mother who raised me to believe that *'no one will ever listen to a woman if a man is not in the room.'* I think her way of thinking encapsulated my need to fulfill the male requests, whether it be in regards to household chores, where it was a woman's job to ensure that the house is clean and the meals are ready to go, to always supporting the man before ourselves.

I lived my life like Cinderella when growing up in Burnaby. My mom raised me to clean the bathrooms and house at nine years old. My sister got to stay pretty and dainty while I did the dirty work. I would have to make sure that the house was clean before my mom would get home from work and have a warm meal on the table. I tried my best, but I wanted to be a kid too, without the responsibilities—no success. I was being groomed to one day cater to my own husband.

This went on for the duration of my childhood years and into my adult life until I finally moved out. As we got older, my mom, sister, and I worked together. We made sure that the lunches were made for everyone's workdays, that dinner was cooked, and that the house was clean.

It would not matter if my dad and my brother were out drinking or made a mess because guess what, they were not expected to raise a hand to do the work! And why would they? As modern as my mom was to the external world, to her own kids, and herself she was backwards. Women were expected to do the household chores, while the men 'provided' and did what they wanted to after work.

I would spend hours making sure the bathrooms and floors were pristine. Then comes along my good old brother, 'no f-s given, privileged attitude, golden child syndrome, makes a mess in every room and no one can hold him accountable—firstborn child always a victim.'

I made a vow to myself that I would never cater to a man the way that I have had to my entire life—to cook and clean. There is so much more to life than that. I promised myself that I would not let the man wear the pants but, instead, I would.

That way no one could ever tell me that I could not do something or try to dictate my life. I would be independent and in control of my own needs.

All I know is, that I did not want to live the same life as my mom. She cannot function or do anything unless my dad is okay and fed. It does not matter how badly he treats her; she will always be back in the kitchen to cater to him. Partly, because of the cultural role of being a devout Indian wife but more importantly being blinded by love.

I will never forget the day when my mom took a many-years pause in my life. It was the day that my dad punched me in the head because I was trying to wake up my sister to get her to sleep in her own room. My Prince George family was visiting at the time, and of course, my dad had had too much to drink and was frustrated with them being there. So once again, the frustration came out on me.

My mom took my dad and me into the bathroom to ask if he had hit me. You have to wonder if she honestly did not know what he was up to when she went to work. Did she not know how abusive he was to me, or was she that naïve and stupid as to believe all his stories? I cannot remember the rest of the conversation between him and her, but I know that he slapped her. And I remember her turning to me saying, 'I will never stand up for you again.'

As I write this, my eyes are filled with tears. For years, I lived with that. How could a mother choose her husband over her daughter, one who was just punched by him? Why bring me into this shitty environment? Why could you not have just left me in Prince George? I would still be getting sexually abused there but at least I would be loved and not afraid of when the next physical abuse would come raining down.

I remember confronting my mom about the incident a few years ago and she did not remember the situation at all. So, a statement that broke me and told me that I was not worthy to be stood up for or cared for, had no remembrance. And that is how trauma works. That slap in her face turned into a trauma that she blocked out because she either did not want to remember it, or it just got stored with all the other little traumas that she experienced in her life.

It was my mom who made me fear men and not the situations. She taught me how to be for men. So, I tried to do everything right whenever a man told me to do something in hopes of being treated better, otherwise, I would not be considered worthy.

Chapter Twenty-three
Strong female influences

I come from a family and lineage of strong women. The women on my mother's side are opinionated, self-sufficient, dominant, and both the most beautiful and ugly people I have ever met.

Growing up, my Prince George mom and her daughters have strong personalities that were fluid and demanded their presence to be known. I was raised to understand that women's rights and injustices needed to be discussed and brought forward. And my Prince George dad (the nicest man I knew) let them speak their truth. They influenced my life greatly. And I became aware of how the world should be and of injustices, just not my own. I gained insight on topics that I would not have otherwise learned.

My mom, on the other hand, had a temper like no other but was well defined as a perfectionist. The perfect cook, designer, dresser, wife, you name it, she was it. I learned a lot from my mom about how to do things, like how to present meals and prepare and host parties. But I learned the most in the past few years when we were no longer mother and daughter but peers. I am kind-hearted and too-giving and nice because of my mom. But as much as these qualities do not let you survive in the real world; they are qualities I cherish and practice because the world needs good people. What we do not need are snakes in blankets, like who my Prince George and extended family turned out to be.

As for my sister, sometimes I do not know if I am the older or younger sister. We are only a year apart and we have been best friends for most of it. Part of her wants to live out loud but the other part of her knows how cruel the world can be, and it forces her to close herself off and go into protection mode.

Without these influences, I would not be who I am. Despite the people my Prince George family turned into, I know what it is like to be loved kindly, and what it is like to receive hard love. Both would mould me into the best version of myself, but also a version that would require years of work and letting go.

My mom taught me honesty. She was always a stand-up woman but fell to the dominance of the men in her life: father, brothers, husband, and son. When the sexual abuse came out about my brother, my mom tried to seek resolution from her sister (my Prince George mom), only to be told that it had not happened. She reached out to her seven brothers and sisters, but no one was around to listen.

Choosing sides, they all stuck together with my Prince George family, never loyal, and watching each one of them change faces. Until it happens to them, it does not matter if it happens to anyone else. They all forgot the years of catering my mom and dad had done for them. Why? Because my parents are a bit on the abrasive side while my Prince George parents remained happy-go-ignorant? I suppose justice is blind for a reason.

All family was lost. My dad's brothers and sisters were either too uncomfortable with the situation at hand or were also told that it had not happened. Everyone turned their backs on us, and we were secluded. There was no one to hear our cries or to help seek resolution. They all chose their side and protected my male cousin, the perpetrator.

When I finally came out to my female cousins, part of me became angry about how long it was taking for them to talk to their brother. Initially, my request was not to have my sister involved in the conversation because I did not want her to be upset if she did not hear what she wanted to. And after speaking with her, I regretted my decision. It made sense as to why she wanted to be part of the conversation. She wanted to hear from him as to why he had done it, a conversation that our parents were never privy to. Fearing it was too late, I called my female cousins to have my sister involved in the call.

We also wanted our female cousins to tell their husbands about the situation. That way, their children could be protected, just in case, this comes out down the road with one of their children. Heck, I kept my sexual abuse a secret for how many years?

To this day, I do not know if my female cousins ever did have the conversation with their husbands. I also was not privileged enough to know when the exact date and time the conversation happened between the oldest female cousin and her brother. I was only given a 'few weeks ago' timeline.

I had told my female cousins in May 2021, and this conversation would have occurred four months later. And he (my male cousin) knew this was coming three months prior to that when I had texted him.

STRONG FEMALE INFLUENCES 111

Quite honestly, I do not know if this conversation would have even happened had my female cousins not been coming to visit for two weeks and needed a place to stay. It seems like the longer they knew about my situation, the longer everyone took to deal with it. More lies and 'matter-of-fact' conversations happened between them and not me. This no longer became about me and what I needed to recover. It became about them protecting their parents and making their family a priority. They were trying to figure out how they could make their family work, while my family fell apart.

The last conversation I had with the oldest female cousin was that she wanted her son, the newborn, to have cousins because he would be living abroad in the next few months. What about his aunts? What about us? Once again, my family and I became ostracized.

The youngest female cousin of the two was too traumatized by her own issues, and never got involved. Instead, she sent her son to stay with her brother unattended. Like I said, if it did not happen to them, then it does not matter. Besides, this happened a long time ago. It cannot happen again, right?

And that is when I realized that the strong women who once influenced me in Prince George, and that I forever looked up to had failed me. They had failed me as a sister. They had failed me as a friend. They had failed me as a human being. They had failed me as a young child seeking help and trying to make sure that history would not repeat itself. Instead, they decided to continue to visit their brother, and to let their kids visit without parental supervision. If history does repeat itself, we may never know. But we warned them, my entire family did.

Chapter Twenty-four

Putting in the work

I did a lot of healing work on myself, and it is only six years later that I feel like I am moving past this and healing. I cannot tell you how many books I have read, or how many positive messages I tried to listen to while getting ready for work or before going to bed. But I truly believe that people and things come into your life when you most need them.

My Reiki master introduced me to the Louise Hay book *You Can Heal Your Life* and *The Power Within You*, which I read a few times. These books allowed me to see how my unhealed traumas were affecting both my mental and physical health. Through this newfound knowledge, I was able to see how important it was to start my healing process with the little girl who underwent the traumas themselves, Baby Mila. I was then able to change the ways I chose to cope with my traumas into more positive actions. I learned that

I could use affirmations to change my mindset and manifest a destiny that I never thought possible.

Then, randomly on YouTube©, a man named Sadhguru popped up on the screen. I immediately became captivated by him and started doing the Isha Kriya meditation in the mornings and evenings. It helped to clear my mind and stabilize my body pain. His words of wisdom in his videos encouraged me to be a better version of myself. I thought I had been okay before, but this made me actually look within myself and heal. That way I would be able to share that inner peace and understanding with the world.

My mentor in Prince George introduced me to a book called *Secret Survivors: Uncovering Incest and Its Aftereffects in Women* by E. Sue Blume. I cried immensely while reading this book. This book made me realize the true extent of abuse and how we let that abuse manifest itself in our lives in other ways. It was that book that allowed me to really see what had happened to me. It allowed me to recognize that I no longer needed to be a victim. I was truly a survivor! So, thank you for allowing me to recognize my true potential.

Then Matthew McConaughey came out with *Greenlights*. Truthfully, I already felt like I was living his life in my real life, except that I was drinking, and had probably blacked out for a good portion of it. This book made me recognize the true blessings that are all around us. We just need to take a moment to pause and reflect to see the potential. Life is all about going with the flow. Eventually, abundance will come to you.

The final book that influenced my healing greatly was a book called *The Emotion Code: How to Release Your Trapped Emotions for Abundant Health, Love, and Happiness* by Dr. Bradley Nelson. It focuses on the clearing of emotions and ancestral trauma. For those that do not know what ancestral trauma means, it means that this is trauma that can be passed down to us by our ancestors. Basically, when you are born, you can inherit not only genetics but also any emotions caused by unresolved trauma from your parents and ancestors.

The Emotion Code has a grid of two columns and six rows with corresponding body organs that are attached to emotions. Every time you go through a traumatic experience, your body can store that emotion in a particular organ.

For example, I had a lot of anger towards my dad and my brother. That anger was then stored in my liver. I did not acknowledge the anger in a healthy way or at all. Eventually, it turned into systemic body pain. With the emotion code grid, you can then remove that emotion from your body. Trauma can be vicious, but energy clearing is real, and it works. I wish I had known about this sooner, but like I said, everything comes to us in divine timing. The first time I cleared myself of any emotions, I cleared eleven in one sitting. I think that was my body also saying, 'I just want this to be over already!'

I did not realize that when you are trying to heal, you have to make time. If you do not start the process on your own, the Universe will eventually stop and make you. And at that point, I hope you realize that you need to make some changes. Obviously, you cannot always stop life just to deal with it. I have been fortunate enough to have a stable income and a job that gives me the flexibility to do some of that healing.

Honestly, I think that if I had not stopped temporarily to start dealing with my traumas, life would have stopped me in a more dramatic way. I might have been diagnosed with a terminal prognosis that would have catapulted me to start making changes. However, you always have a choice to make. Do you start the process or do you not? Either way, your life may be cut short, and all the promises and dreams that you had for yourself and your family, will slowly take their last few breaths and become lost dreams.

If I could shine my wisdom on you, it would be to start doing what you love now. Do not wait until life hits you in the face because of your past. When your past traumas slip their way in, do not dismiss them. Recognize them and try your best to work through the traumas. Most importantly, know that you are not alone. Even though it is going to feel like you are—you are not. Your Spirit Guides are always around. Tap into your spiritual connections by meditating or silencing yourself long enough to listen. Your message may come in the means of a lost puppy, birds in the sky, or a song that comes through the speakers.

Slow down and do not try to rush the process. You cannot, no matter how hard you try. Trust. And when you think you have healed, do not be surprised if something else comes up. The Universe is here to help. Just surrender. As scary as it is, surrender and you will be guided with love and light!

Chapter Twenty-five

My soulmate

On August 28th, 2021, I met the man of my dreams. I know that sounds like a romantic movie, but it was not. It was my real life. Finally, a man on a white horse who had come to sweep me off my feet, someone I could see myself falling madly in love with. I found him. Spirit brought us together.

We met online on a dating app. First and foremost, I never thought I would be on one of those. Secondly, I was surprised at how freeing it felt to put yourself out there, despite having either no likes from people you liked or likes from people you were not interested in. It took me a few tries to create my profile and finally go live with it. It was my message to Spirit and the Universe to say, 'I am ready for love.'

I must have been on the app for about a month before coming across him. I am not sure what it was specifically about him that I liked, but for some reason, I was so attracted to him.

Perhaps, it was his 'plate presentation'. I know that is not going to mean much to the average person but for me, that was how I was raised. The food will not taste as good if it is not presented properly. Much like my upbringing, if you look good then no one will know how badly your life may be falling apart. I liked him and he liked me back and we slowly started talking.

The conversation was not even that engaging but he was a Brasilian football fan, just like me. He even wrote Brasil with the 's' and not 'z'. We moved our conversation off the app and onto another social media platform where we could share pictures. I was reluctant, thinking that he wanted me to send scantily clothed pictures, but he was not. It was merely to send me pictures of his plating. I cannot even say that the food looked good to me but, hey, he was trying, and I was into it.

Conversation dried up and we would not talk for another week. I finally messaged and asked if he was just going to keep looking at all my pictures or if he was going to message me to meet? He said he would. Then another week went by. I posted another picture. No response. Then I posted another that night. To my surprise, I finally received a message: 'Those lips'. I took my shot and I said 'Thanks... when are we hanging out?' Life is short and I wanted to move forward on this. I wanted to know why I was so drawn to meeting him. Honestly, if I had had to wait for him to make a move, I think our meeting would have never happened.

The next day, we met at a local pub close to me. I crossed the road and he stepped out of his vehicle. No hugs, straight to the point and we got a table. I suppose when I get nervous, I act like I am in control when, in reality, I have no idea what I am doing. He initiated the conversation and, maybe five minutes into our meeting, a man came to sing with his guitar.

The very first song that he played was my grandfather's funeral song, *Wildflowers* by Tom Petty. If that was not a sign from Spirit that this was the one, then I do not know what was. We then started talking about our upbringings and he told me that his mother passed away. A minute later, a white butterfly appeared and flew between us. That is when he said, 'When she passed away at the funeral the white butterflies were following me.' That was his sign.

He was such a gentleman and I have never been catered to by a man like I was with him. I was taken off guard. And by surprise, before our meal was done, he asked if I would accompany him to get a baby gift for one of his friends. I agreed. But before we could go, I had to go to the bathroom. And out of all the days, I had brought a purse but had forgotten a mask (this was during the coronavirus pandemic). So, I asked him if we could go back to my house first.

When we walked, I felt like I was walking and talking to the male version of myself. He was outgoing and friendly to the strangers on the street. I have never seen anyone do that, especially in the neighborhood that I live in. Typically, it is me going out of my way to smile or say hi to someone. Again, I was taken aback and by surprise. Even our upbringings were similar, with the dynamics of our fathers and siblings. I felt like I had met the one.

And I did what everyone says not to do. I brought him into my house. And like the butterfly that flew between us, I had butterflies all over the walls of my house. Another sign!

We eventually went to pick up his vehicle and go to the store. After that, I made him take me for gelato when we were done, otherwise, he would be on his own to get the gift. He took me all the way to Burnaby for that, only to have my ice cream fall on the ground mid-walk. I guess it was not meant to be. I hope that we made some dog happy!

We eventually got back to my house, and he started losing his grasp of his words and thoughts while looking at my lips. I have never had anyone do that over me before. I brought him inside and we sat on the couch and talked. I felt so comfortable with him like I have never felt with anyone else. I let myself be vulnerable and told him that I really liked him and that I could see a future with him. I just felt so connected to him. He was the one for me.

I do not know what came over us, but I wanted to kiss him, and I know he wanted to do the same—and so we did! The chemistry and passion were unworldly. Had he not said that he should go, it would have continued. I did not want to let him go but I had to. So, before he left, I made him take my number.

Date 2. It did not go as planned. He got off work, slept, woke up, ran errands, and then had to help his grandparents. An early evening hangout did not happen until 19:44 when he finally showed up. My bedtime was at 21:00. I was not the happiest, but I also know what it is like to have to delay plans because your family needs you. So, I could not be mad because I would have done the same thing. However, the new me had boundaries when it came to my family. Unfortunately, I failed to have boundaries with him. I forgot about myself.

He came over. We talked. I felt so comfortable again and I remained vulnerable and open. I told him that I wanted to follow my heart instead of my head. And he told me not to be stupid. Reflecting on it now, maybe I was. But all my life I have followed my head and never listened to my heart. And for the first time ever, I was listening to my heart—and this felt right.

I do not know where we landed after this but either he was in denial of his feelings or was held back by his previous obligations. He left the connection, and I was left alone and abandoned. After our connection ended, I was lost. Whatever this was, it broke me in a way that I have never been broken before. It would take me months to get myself back together.

Chapter Twenty-six

My dreams

On September 22nd, 2021, I started to have dreams. I used to dream before, on and off, but not to the extent that I would wake up feeling exhausted like I had not slept at all. My dream was of him (my soulmate/the man who abandoned our connection). He was laying on the right side of my bed telling me that he loved me and that he was sorry for leaving me like he had. When he left, there was a dried, brown autumn leaf on my pillow.

My dream two nights later was even more bizarre. I dreamt that my mom, sister, and I received a call to come wash my deceased grandfather's body. So, we went to do it. The house we went to was a house that I had never seen before. All the bedrooms had dark, wood furniture with sky-blue sheets. When we entered the house, I saw my grandfather's feet through the crack of the door. The rest of his body was covered with a white sheet.

At some point, my mom had gone upstairs, and my sister asked me to go get her because my sister wanted to go home. It was only then that I realized whose house, we were in. I went to find my mom and she was standing by the dresser talking with his (my soulmate's) mother. I recognized her from the picture he had shown me. Later, when I was washing dishes, she came downstairs with my mom to give me a white gold infinity bracelet that folded into itself. Unable to take it directly from her, she left it on the corner of the table for me.

Then on September 29th, I dreamt again. This time, of him (my soulmate) and I together. We were kneeling in front of my grandfather. My grandfather was giving us his blessings. After that, his mother came to give us her blessings too.

I remember being so lost after these dreams. Why was I having these dreams of his (my soulmate's) mother and why were she and my grandfather showing up together but not together? I had so many questions and I felt like I was going delusional.

I booked an appointment with my trusted intuitive guide. And on October 3rd, 2021, I received some of the clarity I needed. She said that he (my soulmate) and I had been together in a past life. She said that he had left not because of me, but because of all the men in his life who had abandoned him. It was what he knew.

I asked her if I felt this way about our connection if he (my soulmate) also felt the same way. She said it was possible but also maybe not because if he felt it then he would not have left you the way he did. Prior to our session ending, I finally had to ask if the dreams I was having were real. She confirmed that they were. His mother was actually visiting me and that they had blessed us because we had been married in a previous life.

With a million questions still on my mind, was his (my soulmate's) mother trying to tell me that she accepts me for her son? And if she is visiting me then is she visiting him too? I was spooked. After the session, the dreams started again. On October 4th, 2021, his mother came, and I apologized. I told her that I was sorry that I could not make it work with her son and that it would be up to him if he wanted it to work. She told me 'It is okay' and gave me a hug and a kiss on my forehead.

Then, on October 5th, 2021, I dreamt that he (my soulmate) and I met in a hockey rink with no ice to talk. He again told me how sorry he was. His mother was there too but was sitting by herself on the sidelines, watching. The next day, I wrote her a long letter telling her how thankful I was for meeting her and for all her kindness and gifts. It was my letter to say goodbye to her and her son.

The following day, during my meditation, I saw her (my soulmate's mother) sitting behind my three Spirit Guides. I was concerned, to say the least. First, she had been visiting me in my dreams and now she was sitting in my meditation field.

Later that night, when I meditated again, I saw her (my soulmate's mother). This time, she was sitting with my Spirit Guides. She had incorporated herself in with them. I did not feel scared by her presence, but I was just so confused as to why she was here when her son was not. Was she trying to bring us back together? Should she not be looking after him and his sisters, and not a girl that had just met her son?

The next day, I messaged my intuitive guide and she said that his (my soulmate's) mother was there to help me with this journey, at least for a little while.

And that is what I mean, you never know who or when someone is going to show up in your life to help you or guide you. Typically, we only think of our human connections, but our human connections can lead us to our spiritual connections.

Spirit finds us when we open ourselves up enough to receive their message. Our Spirit Guides come to us when we need them. So, in my current journey, his (my soulmate's) mother is with me to support me and shower me with her unconditional love. I think my process of trying to give myself closure with him has been that much harder because of her presence. Now, I embrace it. When I am struggling with my broken moments, I can call on her to help console me and guide me to my higher self. And if he comes back into my life—boy, do I have stories for him!

When I had first met him (my soulmate), I had felt like I was on my last bit of healing, while he had not even started his journey of processing his mother's death or acknowledging or forgiving his father for his past traumas. So, for someone you feel so connected with or who is a soulmate, they may not be so in this lifetime. When we have not healed, we are not meant to come into alignment.

He (my soulmate) and I had to meet, maybe to expedite his healing and to give closure to mine. We both had to take this forced break because Spirit knew that we were not at our highest caliber to start a fulfilling and nurturing relationship. I know we do not understand or see the bigger picture right away, but eventually, we can figure it out with their help.

Maybe, one day, he (my soulmate) and I will meet again. Otherwise, I am accepting this meeting as someone that I needed to encounter. I send him all the love and light he needs to heal and to move forward in this beautiful life, even if it is not with me.

Chapter Twenty-seven
Find what makes you happy

Healing is hard. It breaks you and it makes you think. It challenges you to come to terms with your past struggles. It is sometimes easier to avoid the healing part and to drown your mind out with a movie or a stiff drink. That is why so many people remain in their 'own' shit and keep repeating history.

Even when I thought I was on the verge of healing or partially working on what I thought I needed to, I used liquor. I used liquor to make me open up and talk about situations that I would not otherwise have had enough courage to talk about.

For the most part, I was that happy-go-lucky drinker. But put me behind the wheel and take me to the liquor store for a cold pack and things would sometimes get too real. I would laugh. I would cry. Drinking in the sun gave me a reason to drink. It became a hobby. It did not matter the day of the week. If it was sunny, then you knew what was going to be happening. Not every sunny day, like my brother, but enough of them to realize that I needed to stop living like I was in a small town.

When I cut out liquor completely, I needed to find new passions. The old me had wanted to be on *Saturday Night Live*. I had practiced doing voices and acting in high school dramas. I had shined on stage and people had remembered me. Then high school had ended, and so had my dreams of acting. I needed to go to school so that I could get a real job.

I taught dance as a side hustle when I moved to Prince George for post-secondary school with my sister. But that would eventually stop when my Prince George mom tried to make her dance school more important than our careers.

Besides drinking and dancing, I did not have a lot of outlets. It was what you did in small towns. I eventually picked up a summer of hard liquor and cigars until I cigared myself out. I hung out with friends, but nothing was ever fulfilling. The only thing in my life that seemed to stay consistent was my love for music.

FIND WHAT MAKES YOU HAPPY

When I listened to music, nothing else mattered. I listened to it, and I was completely absorbed in it. Music would eventually lead me down the path of healing. It opened me up in my Reiki practices, meditations, and dance. Music can be found in all forms, from the birds chirping, to the wind blowing, to the sirens passing by. You just need to be open to listen and be available to fall into its endless possibilities and messages.

Chapter Twenty-eight
How I met my Spirit Guides

I never knew that I had Spirit Guides. All my life, I had thought I was facing all my situations alone. I knew that I had always been interested in the supernatural world but that is where it had ended.

During my nightshifts at the hospital, I used to go ghost hunting through the basements on my breaks with security. I even got an app that would tell me if there were ghosts nearby. And depending on how close they were, their colours on the screen would change.

A few years later, I went to New Orleans for two weeks with my sister to go ghost hunting. Though most of our excursions were hosted by trained professionals, it was not until we entered a certain museum that I truly believe that entities followed us home. That is when our hunt got real, and my mom had to do some real prayers to rid us of the energy that we had brought back.

I found out that I had Spirit Guides after learning Reiki. My Reiki master put me in touch with an intuitive guide that would explain to me that it felt like I was in a dark room with only one lit candle. Basically, I needed to find myself in the light to illuminate the rest of the room. That is when she told me that I have never been alone and that I have Spirit Guides that had been with me from the beginning. She said that they were sorry that they could not help me back then because those had been experiences I had needed to face on my own. But they were ready to help now. At the time, I did not know how to connect with my Spirit Guides other than to journal and continue to read my self-help books.

My second encounter also came from the same intuitive guide. This time, she told me that one of them was ready for me to meet them. We assigned his name as Jacob. He was here to help me restore my faith and trust in men since I had lost my trust in them a long time ago. At first, it was a shock because, all my life, I have devoted my time to surround myself with strong women. It all made sense though. So, slowly, I started to develop a relationship with Jacob, although I was reluctant to start the connection. But learning to trust takes time. Eventually, I would learn that I had three more Spirit Guides.

In pursuit of gaining a closer connection with my Spirit Guides, and since I was finding it difficult to meditate. I purchased my first deck of oracle cards, not to predict my future but to communicate with Spirit on what I needed to do to reach my higher self.

Oracle and tarot cards are tools that can be used to reach new levels of self-awareness.

Chapter Twenty-nine

Surrender

Surrender yourself to the universe. Surrender all the parts of you that are not helping you reach your higher self. Illuminate yourself with love and light. Acknowledge your dark self or shadow parts, and learn to work with them so that they too can be illuminated.

Trust. Trust in yourself. Trust to believe in what is in front of you even if you do not know what that is. The universe will provide. Find the forgiveness in your heart for yourself. Know that whatever happened was not your fault. Forgive those who have hurt you. Learn to love again. Love yourself inside and out. Look in the mirror and into your eyes. Confess your undying love to you for you! Scream it from the mountain top or inside your car while you drive!

The more you say it to yourself or write it down, the more you will start to believe it. Find the things that you love to do, and then do them wholeheartedly. And do things that do not particularly make you happy, and try to do them with love and passion. You might just find something satisfying about the situation or yourself.

Love. Send love to past situations that have wronged you. Send love to present situations that need it. Send love to the people who are no longer in your life. Because at some point, they were there to teach you a lesson—good or bad. Send love to wherever you think it needs to go.

What you put out comes back to you ten-folds. So be kind to yourself and others. Remember that you are not the only one hurting or going through something. Trust in the higher powers and surrender. Take three deep breaths in and then let it go, each time doing a little more. Breathe in love and breathe out all that no longer serves you. You are love. Just trust and believe. You are being guided; just listen!

Chapter Thirty

The Moon

Back when I was going through my acute healing stage, I wish that I had learned about the phases of the moon. Or at the very least known about the full moon. The full moon is all about releasing all that is no longer serving you. It is a time when you have the ability to just let go.

When I initially learned about the full moon, it was when I was working frontline as a nurse. What I learned was that it was the time when people go crazy, and I do not mean the good kind of crazy either. It is like their inner werewolf comes out, except they do not grow teeth or fangs. Instead, they become critter-like and sometimes aggressive. In general, they just act strange. Originally, I just thought it affected the patients, especially the older population. But then I realized that it affected everyone, including the hospital staff. Practices that should have been second nature went out the window, and people would forget what they were doing.

I got into the moon within the last year. It was only after someone told me that the moon should not be something you feared but embraced. Western society has made us believe that night is associated with darkness and evil. However, it is completely the opposite. If you think about it, the sun lights our way during the day and the moon illuminates everything that we need to see at night. A cool blue or white hue, the moon will reflect light on the darker parts of ourselves that requires healing.

Now when I see the moon, I think of all the dark parts that I carry and the things that I want to release from my life. I use the moon to therapeutically release all that is no longer helping me reach my higher self. For me, it was my ego. My inability to let go and to forgive. It was my anger and rage. It was my anxiety and fears.

When you release things from yourself, it is not going to be an easy or fast process. But for some reason, when I choose to release these things during the full moon, I feel like anything that I was having trouble releasing before becomes much more fluid. It is like the moon somehow shines its light on everything, engulfs what I am struggling with, and puts light into the situation.

THE MOON

The next day, I feel like it is easier to deal with things and the burden has been lifted, even if it is not entirely, but enough to lessen the load.

For a long time, I neglected to embrace the moon out of fear and because of the negative connotations attached to it. But, in reality, the moon is our blessing. It illuminates what we do not always choose to see when the sun shines. It casts light on areas of ourselves that need cleansing or purification. Without the moon, we would not have the balance of Ying and Yang. Ultimately, if we did not have one, then we would not have the other.

Write your letters of forgiveness and release them into the midnight sky. Let your fears and anxiety melt away as you engage in forgiveness and light energy. May you feel renewed and blessed by the cool white light grazing across your skin. A chance to break down. A chance to rebuild. A chance to change for the greater good and for yourself.

Chapter Thirty-one

Anger (Part 2)

Remember when I said an apology might not be something you truly need in order to forgive and move on? When I wrote that, I honestly meant it. Because in reality, who is going to give you that apology without having to admit that they did something wrong?

Perhaps it was the dream that I had on the night of January 17th, 2022, the full moon of the wolf. Before going to bed, I asked Spirit to help me heal and see what I was still holding onto. So, I dreamt. I dreamt that I found a pair of scissors. And that male cousin who had sexually abused me all those years ago was standing there with his wife, talking to his older sister.

I felt anger and I felt the rage boil in my blood while he stood there. Never acknowledging my presence, just talking like nothing had happened. How badly I wanted to use those scissors as a weapon like he had used me for all those years. But I did not.

With my hands shaking, I left the room to let my fury subside. Even in my dream, he was not worth the revenge. He was not worth it. He was nowhere close to being worth anything. All the happy memories we had had together were gone. Happy memories turned into sadness and grey nothingness.

That message that I had sent him on June 24th, 2021, the one he chose not to respond to, and the one that I finally felt a release from, still harboured so much anger. I think from that full moon until the January 17th, 2022, full moon, I have been unknowingly storing this anger. When I thought I had forgiven him, I did not. And maybe at the time, I had. But the trauma kept creeping up. And I kept telling myself that it would take time to heal.

For seven years he had sexually abused me and now he could not send a message of apology? Or at the very least tell his sisters how sorry he was? I have dealt with his secret for the past thirty-two years, from what I can remember. But what if the sexual abuse had happened before I was two years old? I can only remember from two years old and onwards.

Furthermore, what would have happened if my parents had not forced me to move back home with them when I was nine years old? How far would the abuse have gone then?

As I look at my childhood pictures, it is hard to recognize the little girl standing there. With all her smiles and cries, you would never know what was going on behind closed doors. I feel ashamed and guilty for not speaking up about this abuse. And it seems like the longer that I hold onto it, the more pain it is causing. How do I tell my parents? How do I tell my brother? I sit here and let the tears run down my face and I pray. I pray and hope for a better outcome to this pain.

I will probably never get an apology from this male cousin who sexually abused me. He is forever a coward for preying on such an innocent child, regardless of how young he had been when he had started the abuse. He knew better, especially to go after two siblings or any young child at that. And he was still a coward to this day for not being able to apologize to me when we were in Prince George, or when we had both left to go home after our grandfather's cremation.

No apologies. No acknowledgement, as if the entire seven years of my life were a fictional tale. I just hope that he is not doing the same to his own kids. And that his wife, who chooses to stand beside him, knows what he did, not once but twice.

This is no longer my secret. This is his. This is his burden that he can live with every single day of his life. Whether or not people tie him to this book—I have no idea. Either way, karma has his address, along with all the people who continue to help him conceal this secret. Everything that goes around eventually comes around. Light always triumphs over darkness.

REST IN PEACE to this chapter of my life. I am no longer my anger and rage. I am LOVE and LIGHT. I SURVIVED!

Chapter Thirty-two

My intention and hope

Every morning I wake up, I sit in bed and do my meditation to say thank you to Spirit for allowing me to be alive. Then I brush my teeth and get ready for the day. Once I leave my room, I go to my prayer area and pray again to say thank you. I pray that everyone in this world finds forgiveness for themselves and for those that have hurt them. That way, they can move forward in their journey.

I then pray for the animals because, like small children, they do not have a voice, and are dependent on humans to either take care of them or not destroy the land that they reside on to lay, eat, and procreate. I then pray again and say thank you for allowing myself to find the forgiveness in my own heart so that I can move into healing light and love energy. I give thanks for guiding me on this journey. I surrender all that I cannot control to Shirdi Sai Baba, the

Universe, Mataji, Ganeshji, and into the Divine hands. I ask my Spirit Guides to guide me in the right direction of abundance, light, joy, good health, happiness, success, and more.

My hope. I am not sure if this book will ever irradicate future sexual, physical, emotional, or mental abuse, but I hope that it reaches someone that has gone through any kind of trauma. Know that there is hope and that you are not alone. These abuses are more common than you think. It is just that no one openly talks about them. You do not have to keep living within your trauma; there is life outside of it. A life full of abundance and love! Just know that you will survive this. You CAN survive this! I hope that this book allows you to do just that. Eventually, you can say with pride and a smile 'I SURVIVED.'

After all, we are just fragments in this world. But with each fragment, we can collectively make this world a better place to live in for both ourselves and others.

I am sending you all so much love and light on your journey of healing.

With all my love and the Divine's grace,

Mila

Chapter Thirty-three

My sincere gratitude

Thank you to **everyone** who has come into my life to either teach me something or to allow me to come to terms with a situation.

Thank you to my **mom** for your unconditional love and for teaching us the difference between right and wrong. Thank you for providing us with all of life's gifts. I love you, always.

Thank you to my **dad**. As constantly as we fight, I have learned a lot despite everything. It has made me stand that much taller and work that much harder for everything that I want.

Thank you for teaching us that we deserve the best in life.

To **Rajeev**, my brother. Maybe if life had not thrown us the curve balls that it did, life would have been a lot different between us. May this book give you the light and peace that you need to finally heal.

Thank you, **Shelly**, my sister, for being there through the thick and thin. No words can express how I feel about you. I am so glad that we have had another lifetime together to fulfill and live our dreams—BIG!

Lucky! As hard as it was for us to let you go. It forced us to make room in our hearts, so that we could fill it with even more love for others.

MY SINCERE GRATITUDE

Lincoln! Thank you for your big hugs and warm kisses. You opened up our hearts to the bigger possibilities of life and have taught us that life does not have to be difficult—just breathe and let things go. Abundance will come.

Hunter! Thank you for teaching us beauty and grace. Thank you for coming into our lives and teaching us how to love. And thank you for teaching us that we should never stop searching for the truth or the meaning of life!

To **Renee**, I am truly grateful for meeting you when I did. You helped me find my initial voice when I was first embarking on my journey of healing.

To **Jackie**, for allowing me to heal and for working through my journey with me! I do not know if I would have progressed and healed without your constant support. When I did not think that I could heal anymore, you came and showed me that I could. I thank you from the bottom of my heart.

To **Sabrina**, for being the conduit for Spirit and for relaying their messages to me! Thank you for guiding me in the right direction of what it was that I needed to do, to be better and to reignite my light. Thank you for starting my process.

To **Ann Therese**, thank you for encouraging me to speak my truth.

To **Jimmy**, thank you for all of your love and for staying level-headed and grounded throughout this whole process. Justice will eventually find its way through!

MY SINCERE GRATITUDE

To **Asha Auntie**, for giving me my initial gift of healing with Reiki, and for showing me that I have the ability to heal myself and others. Thank you for helping me see what I was not able to.

My **Wael**. Thank you for coming into my life when you did and for flipping it upside down and around. I needed that to heal and to reach my higher self. Thank you for bringing your **mother** into my life as unintentional as it was. We were destined to meet, and I am forever thankful for gaining another mother and confidant.

Dearest **Spirit—thank you!** I could not and would not have been able to create this book without you! Nor would I have been able to stand where I am today without your continual guidance and love. Thank you, thank you, thank you! I am forever grateful and blessed!

Epilogue

As I reflect on my life on how far I have come, it amazes me that I was once that small girl who was abused for all those years—and I still made it through! It seems like a lifetime ago that I even went through it. I still deal with the repercussions every day, but each day it becomes easier, and the memories become more distant. There are times when I am still triggered by certain incidents, but they are becoming few and far between.

My truth is finally out. Not only in this book for the world to read, but for my family. With the encouragement of my sister and my Spirit Guides, I gained the emotional strength to tell my parents and my brother.

Sometimes, I still wonder what pushed me to that moment of truth. I suppose, part of me did it for my own healing, and the other part was to show my family that it is possible to persevere in the midst of this turmoil.

I know I ripped open each one of their wounds by telling them what happened. But ultimately, I could not keep living with this secret. Had I not spoken about my truth, my health would have likely deteriorated even more, and I would not have been able to move forward in life.

For a second time, my parents, and my brother were forced to deal with what they thought was over. And for a second time, they tried to seek the justice they never received when my brother came out about his own sexual abuse seven years ago from the same male cousin.

Even though there should have been more hope this time around, everyone still turned a blind eye. An uncomfortable topic that no one wanted to navigate through—unless it was solely affecting them.

My Prince George family is no longer my family. Each member now knows the truth about what happened to me as a baby. And as much as I thought I was part of their family as a daughter, sister, and cousin, I was reminded that I was not. Blood is thicker than water. Their son and their brother was worth protecting more than my brother and me, even though the sexual abuse happened under their watch.

EPILOGUE

My brother and I will never get our time back for all the tears and efforts we have had to put into healing. More importantly, we will never get our childhood or innocence back. All lost time.

If no resolution can be sought out for my family, then maybe this book will give them the justice and peace that they truly desire.

And to those still dealing with these internal conflicts. You may never receive the justice that you need. At some point, you are going to have to wipe your hands clean. Forgive and move on, if not for them then for yourself.

Justice will come for those who have hurt us eventually. If not in this lifetime, then the next. Above all else, never give up your fight or ability to speak your truth and to stay in your power. Healing will eventually come with time. Just surrender and keep believing.

Acknowledgments

I want to say a special thank you to my mom, sister, and Lincoln for all of your unbiased love and support during this entire process! I know it has not been easy, but I would not have been able to express my words with the clarity that this book needed. With your help, I was able to truly create a full picture of the situations and people involved. Thank you for understanding that my story was not just meant for my healing, but for all the little girls and boys who have grown up and are still stuck in their traumas.

Thank you, Spirit, for showing me that I could find healing by sharing my story. Only you could have foreseen me writing this entire book by hand with only a clipboard, stack of paper, and pen! And only you know how difficult my healing journey has been with my pain, tears, vivid dreams, and sleepless nights. Thank you for allowing me to experience the life lessons that I have. It was through those lessons that allowed me to find the peace and light I needed—and to find my purpose. You knew that my life was meant to be shared. Thank you for helping me find my shine! I am unbreakable!

Mother Willow, thank you for showing me a strength within myself that I did not know I had. A strength that I would need so that I could face the trial and tribulations of my traumas. The strength you instilled in me allowed me to wake up each day and find the power to forgive and heal. You showed me how strong I truly am, and that I have a voice that deserves to be heard. No longer will I choose to play it safe and stay quiet. Thank you for allowing me to find the words to write my story!

Mom (my soulmate's mother) thank you for bringing hope back into my life. And thank you for helping me put myself back together. Mom, it is because of you that I still have hope that love exists and that there are people out there that want to make this world better. Thank you for helping me gain a deeper connection with the spiritual world—more than I ever thought possible!

Grampa! Thank you for being my support in your afterlife, and for letting me know that I deserve happiness and love. I know you are doing all you can to make miracles happen. I hope you are being less stubborn wherever you are! I love you!

Jacob, thank you for allowing me to find the confidence and self-love I needed to share my story. You have been with me the longest and I am so appreciative of your unconditional love and guidance. Thank you for protecting me always!

Esmeralda, thank you for reminding me how to laugh and dance again. Most importantly, thank you for allowing me to learn to let go and release my past traumas and burdens. And thank you for allowing me to embrace life. It is only now that I enjoy the beauty that surrounds me and I am so grateful!

From the beginning to the end, thank you to my baby self, Baby Mila for helping me find me again and for allowing us to work together to find our purpose! I am truly sorry for neglecting you for all those years, but we found each other again and I am never letting you go! I love you more and more each day—forever and always!

About Author

Mila Sharma is a Registered Nurse in British Columbia, Canada. As a true Piscean, she has always been motivated by the art of writing, dancing, drawing, and stargazing. From the age of twelve, she always knew she was destined to write a book. Little did she know that her first book would be one that showcased the hardships of her life. Through perseverance, she has excelled in both her nursing career and healing practices by completing her Level 1 and 2 Reiki certifications. She plans on becoming a Reiki Master, now that this book is published! With this, she hopes that her continual work with energy and her words will provide the necessary love, light, and forgiveness that this world desperately needs.

www.ingramcontent.com/pod-product-compliance
Lightning Source LLC
Chambersburg PA
CBHW050027130526
44590CB00042B/2030